Assembly Language Reimagined

Programming the Intel x64 Microprocessor in Linux

John Schwartzman

Apress®

Assembly Language Reimagined: Programming the Intel x64 Microprocessor in Linux

John Schwartzman
Ellicott City, MD, USA

ISBN-13 (pbk): 979-8-8688-1723-6 ISBN-13 (electronic): 979-8-8688-1724-3
https://doi.org/10.1007/979-8-8688-1724-3

Managing Director, Apress Media LLC: Welmoed Spahr
Acquisitions Editor: James Robinson Prior
Development Editor: Jim Markham
Coordinating Editor: Gryffin Winkler

Cover image designed by Freepik (www.freepik.com)

Distributed to the book trade worldwide by Springer Science+Business Media New York, 1 New York Plaza, New York, NY 10004. Phone 1-800-SPRINGER, fax (201) 348-4505, e-mail orders-ny@springer-sbm.com, or visit www.springeronline.com. Apress Media, LLC is a Delaware LLC and the sole member (owner) is Springer Science + Business Media Finance Inc (SSBM Finance Inc). SSBM Finance Inc is a **Delaware** corporation.

For information on translations, please e-mail booktranslations@springernature.com; for reprint, paperback, or audio rights, please e-mail bookpermissions@springernature.com.

Apress titles may be purchased in bulk for academic, corporate, or promotional use. eBook versions and licenses are also available for most titles. For more information, reference our Print and eBook Bulk Sales web page at http://www.apress.com/bulk-sales.

Any source code or other supplementary material referenced by the author in this book is available to readers on GitHub: https://www.apress.com/gp/services/source-code.

If disposing of this product, please recycle the paper

2 Kate, 4 Everything.

Table of Contents

About the Author .... **ix**

About the Technical Reviewer .... **xi**

Acknowledgments .... **xiii**

Preface .... **xv**

Chapter 1: Using BIOS Services **1**

What Is the BIOS? 1

Getting Started 1

The Anatomy of a Makefile 5

Running the DDD Debugger 10

Activities 13

Chapter 2: Extending BIOS Services **15**

A Brief Introduction to Boolean Logic Gates 20

Representation of Numbers in the Computer 22

The DDD Debugger 26

Activities 28

Chapter 3: Prefer glibc over BIOS Calls, uname Reprise **29**

The Stack 29

The C Calling Convention 31

The Linker 32

Data Sections 37

The uname2.asm Program 37

The os-distro.sh Shell Script 38

Activities 40

Chapter 4: Passing Information to a Program on the Command Line 43

The DDD Debugger 52

Activities 52

Chapter 5: Using Macros and Passing Arguments on the Stack 55

More About Macros 62

Activities 64

Chapter 6: Conditional Compilation and Conditional Build 67

The DDD Debugger 74

Activities 75

Chapter 7: Recursion 77

Activities 85

Chapter 8: Using Floating Point Registers 87

Activities 92

Chapter 9: The commaSeparate Utility 95

Activities 103

Chapter 10: The hhmmss Utility Program 105

Activities 112

Chapter 11: Creating and Using a Shared Library 113

Activities 120

Chapter 12: Sorting an Array of Integers 123

Activities 135

Chapter 13: Sorting an Array of Strings 139

Activities 150

Searching an Array of Strings 152

Activities 156

Chapter 14: Finding, Reading, and Selecting File and Directory Metadata 157

Activities 163

Chapter 15: Creating and Sorting a Linked List....................165

Activities....................181

Chapter 16: Reading and Sorting File and Directory Information by Reading Directories....................183

Activities....................212

Chapter 17: Reading File and Directory Information with the Help of the Linux Shell Scripting Language, BASH....................215

Activities....................219

Afterword....................221

Appendix A: Installing the Software....................223

Glossary....................227

Endnotes....................233

Index....................235

About the Author

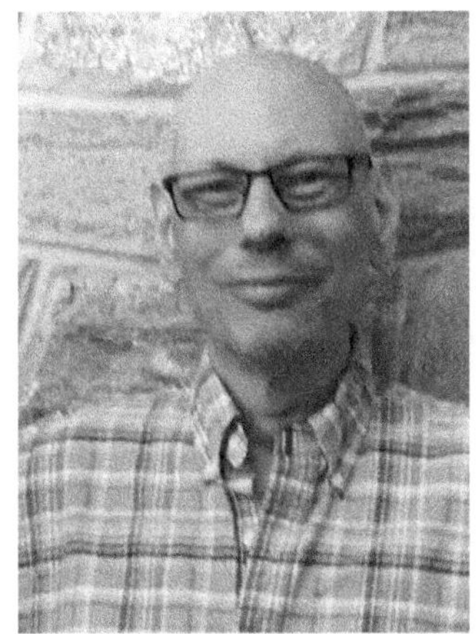

John Schwartzman is a hardware/software engineer with over 40+ years of industry and teaching experience of hands-on coding and design. He has managed groups in tech companies large and small and is a regular writer for *Linux Magazine* and *Linux Format*.

About the Technical Reviewer

Seth Kenlon is a sysadmin, open source and free culture advocate, Java and Lua programmer, game designer, and tabletop gamer. He has worked at tech startups, at Weta Digital on movies, and is currently employed at Red Hat/IBM as a professional Linux geek.

Acknowledgments

Thanks are gratefully given to Gryffin Winkler and his review team at Apress. Jim Markham provided much helpful feedback.

Preface

I started writing this book with the idea that knowledge of assembly language programming would be useful to software engineers. I finished this book with the firm conviction that knowledge of assembly language programming is essential for every serious student of computer science. Writing this book has made me a better computer engineer. I think that working through this book will elevate and inform your own programming.

The emphasis in this book is on what the processor is doing while a high-level structured computer language program is being run. The book describes what a computer can, and can't, do and how it can solve problems with the help of software. This book applies to the entire field of computer science and not just the somewhat narrow area of assembly language programming.

What Is Assembly Language?

Assembly language is a low-level programming language: it's specific to a particular processor. It is used to program a specific processor at the hardware level. Compilers for languages like C, C++, Pascal, FORTRAN, BASIC, COBOL, Python, Go, Rust, etc., understand assembly language because that's what they use to break down a high-level language program into its equivalent low-level assembly language instructions. Assembly language is relevant to all high-level computer languages.

C++ is used to create many different programming languages. The C++ compiler strings together lots of assembly language instructions to do the actual work. Every kind of program ultimately executes machine language on the computer hardware.

Why Learn Assembly Language?

Learning assembly language won't make you a faster programmer. It won't enable you to create portable, write-once, run-anywhere programs. It's not new. It's not object oriented. So why learn it? The answer is that it will make you a better programmer. By learning just what a processor can and can't do, you gain a deeper understanding of computer science.

A processor doesn't just perform arithmetic; it also performs *Boolean* logic operations. Understanding Boolean logic operations teaches you about the Boolean logic gates inside the central processing unit (*CPU*) of your computer. It shows you the way in which your programs use these logic gates to make decisions about program flow. Understanding this will make you a more capable and versatile computer engineer.

What Are Mnemonics?

Mnemonics are simple names or abbreviations given to numeric machine language instructions. Assembly language is simply machine language with mnemonics substituted for numeric op codes. A processor contains hundreds of numeric instructions (op codes). Assembly language allows you to write programs using mnemonics like ADD, SUB, MOV, JMP, AND, OR, and so on. A mnemonic like MOV (move) can indicate many different types of moves. We can move a number from a memory location to a *register* (a named, very fast, 64-bit memory location located inside the *CPU*), from a register to a memory location, from one register to another, from an immediate data value specified in the program to a register, etc. These are known as addressing modes, and they are determined by the *arguments* supplied with a *mnemonic* in an assembly language statement. We use mnemonics because, as you can imagine, they're a lot easier to remember than numeric op codes.

What Is Embedded Programming?

In embedded programming, we regulate voltages and currents in a physical machine (hardware) that contains a CPU and memory. In many cases, a hardware device may have time constraints associated with it. When reading from the read sensor of a spinning disk, you only have a small interval of time after you process a bit before the next bit arrives and must be processed. The bits are stored serially on the disk. As bit rates increase, the interval of time between bits falls and the software must respond more quickly than before. At some point, a high-level language will fail to respond quickly enough to reassemble the bits into bytes, and assembly language must be employed in its stead.

Assembly language is very useful in embedded programming because it is closer to the physical machine than a high-level language. It is very easy to include assembly language modules with high-level language modules to facilitate the development of embedded systems.

What Are High-Level Computer Languages?

High-level languages make programs portable. They enable you to program without worrying about the low-level details of how a CPU works, and they don't appear to care what CPU is inside your computer. They provide the *abstraction* that lets you think about problems at a higher level. Every computer must, however, have high-level language compilers written specifically for the CPU of that computer. The executable code is written for one specific CPU, only.

Object-oriented languages like C++, Java, C#, Python, and so on are "higher" high-level languages that enable you to incorporate the problem-domain into your program. The programs you create with an object-oriented language "understand" your application's problem-domain and not just the generic algorithms used to operate on data. For example, a student program written for a university will have a function to compute grade point average. But assembly language is at the heart of every high-level language. The machine code which runs on your computer is created by the assembler, which is inside every high-level language compiler.

Why Study the Intel x86_64 64-Bit Microprocessor?

A great number of the computers in homes, offices, factories, schools, and laboratories employ Intel x86_64 CPUs, so in this book we're writing assembly language in the Intel x86_64 dialect. We're using the Linux operating system and so we start by writing a couple of simple assembly language programs that use Linux kernel services. These are low-level services that the operating system makes available to compilers and assemblers. In Chapter 3, we'll begin using the C run-time library (glibc) to write more complicated programs. In many cases, the glibc *methods* are thin wrappers around the Linux kernel services. Although this discussion is restricted to the Intel x86_64 64-bit CPU, it is very easy to transfer a knowledge of assembly language programming to other processors. With other processors, you will encounter slightly different mnemonics, but the basic instructions and addressing modes are identical. In general, we present each example assembly language program with its C or C++ language equivalent.

Why Linux?

This text focuses on the Linux operating system. Linux is an open source, multiuser UNIX-like operating system. It is not tied to a specific manufacturer like Microsoft or Apple. You don't have to pay a licensing fee to use Linux. It is a popular choice for web servers, supercomputers, and higher education.

What Is a Makefile?

The programs we build come in two basic flavors, release and debug. Debug is good for writing and testing. Release mode produces a smaller executable. We use release mode for distribution and debug mode for development.

Release mode programs start from the address of the first instruction in memory, executing each instruction in memory until the last instruction is reached, at which point we return to the BIOS. Debug mode programs can be run just like release mode programs, but they can also be run inside a debugger.

A debugger is a multithreaded program that lets you stop the program under test at critical points and examine the contents of registers, variables, instructions, and memory. It is invaluable for understanding and explaining how a computer program works. It's also invaluable for finding and correcting logic errors in your code.

Syntax errors and typing errors are usually caught in the edit-make cycle, but many logic errors require a debugger and a skilled debugger-user to unravel. A makefile can create both debug and release forms of the executable for you.

This textbook provides a makefile for every chapter. The makefiles will build each example program in release mode or in debug mode. Sometimes you will have to modify the makefile to produce additional executables. Executing the debug or release executable will help demonstrate the concepts of the chapter.

Release mode strips out the debugging information (line number references to the source code) from the final executable file. During the development process, we usually build in debug mode.

Appendix A tells you how to download the editor, assembler, compilers, make utility, debugger, source code, and other tools you'll need to complete the examples and activities in this book.

The Need for Speed

The microprocessor CPU operates on a square wave clock waveform. The clock runs at somewhere around 3G CPS (3 billion cycles per second) on a personal computer, where every clock cycle lasts approximately 0.33 ns (one-third of a billionth of a second per cycle). The speed at which a program runs depends upon which component of the computer is doing the work at the present moment.

The fastest components are the registers inside the CPU. An instruction that moves data from one register to another takes one clock cycle, because all of the action takes place inside the CPU. Moves from a register to memory take longer because we have to wait for the memory address to stabilize on the address bus and data to stabilize on the data bus and for the memory device to be selected. Immediate mode operations like mov rax, 0 (move zero into the rax register) take about the same time as a register to memory transfer. Hard disk to register moves take longer still, since we have to wait for the disk to spin up and to be accessed. Other *IO* (input/output) hardware operations take longer still. The computer does its best by caching program memory in high-speed memory *cache* built into the CPU. It also predicts what future accesses will be needed by caching instructions following a jump. It can load instructions speculatively into *cache* so that it has cached instructions no matter which way the jump goes. Modern CPUs can have many cores, so that instructions can be executed in parallel if the software supports this. Modern CPUs also support pipelining, in which the simultaneous execution of more than one instruction takes place.

Although you can see that the computer itself has multiple methods for increasing program speed, assembly language programming is another way to increase speed. No high-level computer language offers the fine-grained control of assembly language.

CISC vs. RISC

A Complex Instruction Set Computer (*CISC*) like the Intel x86_64 has many complicated instructions that take much longer than a single clock cycle to execute. A Reduced Instruction Set Computer (*RISC*), on the other hand, tends to avoid complicated instructions and strives to execute every instruction in its instruction set in fewer clock cycles than its CISC counterparts. The assumption is that any deficiencies in the instruction set will be taken care of in software.

Assembly language helps achieve the best performance from either architecture.

Practice Makes (Nearly) Perfect

You learn a computer language through constant practice, so I have included many questions and activities in each chapter.

I had a lot of fun writing this textbook. I hope you find it helpful, relevant, and enjoyable! I hope it gives you a more intuitive understanding of high-level structured code.

John Schwartzman

January 2025

CHAPTER 1

Using BIOS Services

What Is the BIOS?

The Basic Input Output System (BIOS) is a non-volatile program burned into read-only memory (ROM). It is available as soon as the computer is powered on. It contains instructions for interfacing to the hardware peripherals as well as instructions for loading the operating system. The BIOS provides a low-level interface to hardware peripherals. The *UEFI (Unified Extensible Firmware Interface)* is a newer open source replacement for the BIOS. When the computer is powered on, all of its intelligence is in the BIOS or the UEFI. As part of the boot process, the operating system is loaded into *RAM (random access memory) and executed by the BIOS or UEFI.*

Getting Started

It has become obligatory to introduce every new programming language with a program that prints “Hello, world!” to the console, so we’ll start there.[1] Listing 1-1 shows the C language code hello.c. Listing 1-2 shows the equivalent assembly language code, hello.asm. Listing 1-3 shows the make file, Makefile, which is used to build (assemble, compile, and link) the two programs in this chapter. Listing 1-4 shows the maketest.sh shell script that is used in every build.

The hello executable is made by compiling and linking hello.asm, which calls two BIOS subroutines to do its work. The a.out executable is made from hello.c and two GNU C library (glibc) subroutines. The Makefile contains instructions to assemble, compile, link, and create these two executable programs.

J. Schwartzman, *Assembly Language Reimagined*, https://doi.org/10.1007/979-8-8688-1724-3_1

Listing 1-1. hello.c

```
// hello.c
// John Schwartzman, Forte Systems, Inc.
// 04/06/2023

#include <stdio.h>            // declaration of printf
#include <stdlib.h>           // defines EXIT_SUCCESS

int main()
{
    printf("\nHello, world!\n\n");
    return EXIT_SUCCESS;
}
```

Listing 1-2. hello.asm

```
;=====================================================================
; hello.asm
; John Schwartzman, Forte Systems, Inc.
; 04/09/2023
;
;======================== CONSTANT DEFINITIONS =======================
LF              equu      10    ; ASCII linefeed character
EXIT_SUCCESS    equ        0    ; Linux apps normally return 0 for success
STDOUT          equ        1    ; destination for SYS_WRITE
SYS_WRITE       equ        1    ; kernel SYS_WRITE service number
SYS_EXIT        equ       60    ; kernel SYS_EXIT service number

;============================ CODE SECTION ===========================
section.text
global _start

_start:
mov             rdi, STDOUT     ; 1st arg to SYS_WRITE - where to write
```

```
lea             rsi, [msg]      ; 2nd arg to SYS_WRITE - what to write
mov            rdx, MSGLEN      ; 3rd arg to SYS_WRITE - how much to write
mov             rax, SYS_WRITE  ; tell BIOS to call SYS_WRITE service
syscall

sub             rax, MSGLEN     ; syscall ret with rax = num bytes written
mov             rdi, rax        ; 1st arg to SYS_EXIT = 0 if MSGLEN char written
mov             rax, SYS_EXIT   ; prepare to call SYS_EXIT
syscall                         ; tell BIOS to call SYS_EXIT service

;====================== READ-ONLY DATA SECTION ======================
section.rodata
msg:  db        LF, "Hello, world!", LF, LF
MSGLEN:         equ         $-msg
;====================================================================
```

Listing 1-3. Makefile for hello

```
########################################################################
#
#    Makefile for hello
#    John Schwartzman, Forte Systems, Inc.
#    04/06/2023
#
#    Commands:  make .release, .make debug, make clean
#               make = make release
#  Requires:  ../maketest.sh
#
########################################################################
PROG  := hello
SHELL := /bin/bash

.release: $(PROG).asm $(PROG).c Makefile
```

```
    @source ../maketest.sh && test .release .debug
    yasm -f elf64 -o $(PROG).obj $(PROG).asm   # hello.asm => hello.obj
    ld $(PROG).obj -o $(PROG)                  # hello.obj => hello
    gcc -O3 $(PROG).c                          # hello.c => a.out

.debug: $(PROG).asm $(PROG).c Makefile
    @source ../maketest.sh && test .debug .release
    yasm -f elf64 -g dwarf2 -o $(PROG).obj $(PROG).asm   # hello.asm =>hello.obj
    ld -g $(PROG).obj -o $(PROG)               # hello.obj => hello
    gcc -g $(PROG).c                           # hello.C => a.out

clean:
    rm -f $(PROG) $(PROG).obj a.out .debug .release
######################################################################
```

Listing 1-4. maketest.sh

```
#!/bin/bash
#########################################################################
# maketest.sh
# John Schwartzman, Forte Systems, Inc. 06/03/2019
#
# A makefile helper script to manage .debug and .release makefiles
# using the same source, object and executable files.
# In Makefile use: @source ../maketest.sh && test .release .debug
#                  @source ../maketest.sh && test .debug .release
# Invoke Makefile with make .release, make .debug
#
#########################################################################
function test()
{
    if [[ ! -f $1 ]]; then
        touch $1;
        rm -f $2;
```

```
    else
        touch $1;
        fi
}
###########################################################################
```

Let's take a closer look at the Makefile now.

The Anatomy of a Makefile

By default, when make looks for the makefile, it tries the following names in order: GNUmakefile, makefile, and Makefile. You can give the makefile any name you like, however, by calling it with 'make -f <name_of_makefile>.' I decided to call all of our makefiles Makefile.

A makefile is primarily composed of targets, file dependencies for targets, instructions to build targets, definitions, and comments. Each target and its dependencies is followed by a tab-character-indented set of instructions for building the target.

The makefile in Listing 1-3 contains two targets: .release, .debug and the pseudo-target, clean. We specify which target we want to build by typing **make .release**, **make .debug** or **make clean** at the shell prompt. (The shell prompt is often called the command line interface, CLI. It is usually the $ character in the console.) If we just type **make** without a target name, the first target (.release) is chosen. Each target is followed by a colon and any file dependencies for the target. The .release target and its list of dependencies is followed by the instructions for building the release versions of hello. The .debug target and its list of dependencies is followed by the instructions for building the debug versions of hello. The clean pseudo-target has no dependencies. It removes any *artifacts* of the build process like hello.obj, hello, a.out, .debug and .release. The name a.out (assembler out) is the default name given to the executable file created by compiling and linking hello.c with gcc.

The build and release targets begin by loading and executing a small bash shell program (../maketest.sh) located in the parent directory of hello. This allows us to use the same names and directories for our release and debug versions of the program. It creates empty files in the default directory named .debug and .release and deletes any existing .release or .debug file.

Our makefile uses YASM (yet another assembler) to assemble our assembly language files into .obj (object) files. Yasm is a rewrite of the NASM assembler in the C language. The makefile uses the Linux ld utility program to link an object file into an executable format. The makefile uses the gcc program to compile and link our C file.

Make executes the instructions to build a target only if the time-date stamp on the target file is older than any of its file dependencies. The target .release will be built if the empty file .release doesn't exist in the working directory or if it does exist and it is older than hello.asm, hello.c, or Makefile. If make tells you that the .release target is up to date and refuses to build, you can always force it to rebuild with the instruction **make -B .release** (or **make .release -B**).

The maketest.sh shell script allows our debug and release outputs to share the same names and directories.

Set the current working directory to the directory where you installed hello.asm. Then type make (or make .release) at the shell prompt in the hello directory and verify that hello.obj, hello, and a.out are created. Hello.obj is the intermediate assembler object file; the linker/loader turns it into an executable file.

```
js@suse-leap-z4:~$ cd Development/asm_x86_64/hello
js@suse-leap-z4:~/Development/asm_x86_64/hello$ make
...
js@suse-tumbleweed-z4:~/Development/asm_x86_64/hello$ ls -lhAF
total 56K
-rwxr-xr-x 1 js js  20K Jan 28 07:22 a.out*
-rw------- 1 js js   78 May  4  2023 .gdb_history
drwxr-xr-x 1 js js  144 Nov 25 04:44 .git/
-rw-r--r-- 1 js js   45 May  4  2023 .gitignore
-rwxr-xr-x 1 js js 8.7K Jan 28 07:22 hello*
-rw-r--r-- 1 js js 1.4K Dec 24 05:35 hello.asm
-rw-r--r-- 1 js js  247 May  4  2023 hello.c
-rw-r--r-- 1 js js  832 Jan 28 07:22 hello.obj
-rw-r--r-- 1 js js  954 Dec 19 12:18 Makefile
-rw-r--r-- 1 js js    0 Jan 28 07:22 .release
drwxr-xr-x 1 js js  140 May  4  2023 .vscode/
js@suse-tumbleweed-z4:~/Development/asm_x86_64/hello$
```

Note that file names in the list returned by ls -lhAF that are followed by an asterisk are executable. Note also that only the owner, "js", has read, write, and execute permissions to the executable files. The members of the group "users" have read and execute permissions. And everyone else has read and execute permissions to these executable files. Only the owner, js, or the superuser, root, can write or delete the source files hello.asm and hello.c or the intermediate file, hello.obj. This security is a basic feature of a multiuser operating system like Linux.

Let's try executing the output files.

Remember that, in Linux, the present working directory (PWD) is not normally in the PATH. We can't just type hello at the shell prompt; we have to type ./hello to specify that we want the shell to execute hello in our present working directory ($PWD = ./).

```
js@suse-leap-z4:~/Development/asm_x86_64/hello$ ./hello

Hello, world!

js@suse-leap-z4:~/Development/asm_x86_64/hello$ ./a.out

Hello, world!
```

The assembly language executable and the C language executable produce the same output. That's encouraging!

The main method of hello.c has two very simple instructions. It calls the C runtime library glibc's printf method to print a constant *string* of characters. It then calls ret EXIT_SUCCESS to return control to Linux. EXIT_SUCCESS is a constant equal to the number 0.

Now let's examine hello.asm.

The program has two sections, one for code (section .text) and the other for data (section .rodata, where .rodata stands for read-only data). We start with some comments (lines 1 through 6) and then some constant declarations (lines 7 through 11).

The text section begins at the label _start (line 18). After Linux loads hello into memory, it will set the CPU's instruction pointer *register* (rip) to the instruction located at the _start label. Then the CPU starts executing the instructions in hello's .text (code) section.

The action begins with the *marshaling* (assembling and making ready for action) of arguments to our first syscall.

Arguments to the Linux kernel are always passed in the same set of six registers. The first argument is passed in rdi, the second in rsi, the third in rdx, the fourth in r10, the fifth in r8, and the sixth in r9. You can pass a maximum of six arguments to a Linux kernel service. All BIOS subroutines look for their arguments in these six registers.

The SYS_WRITE syscall only takes three arguments. The first argument indicates where we want to write. We choose standard out (STDOUT = 1) to indicate that we want Linux to write to the terminal (console). We do this in line 18 with the immediate mode move instruction (mov rdi, STDOUT). This is an immediate mode mov instruction, because STDOUT (1) comes from the program memory space and not from a variable in memory or from another register.

The second argument indicates what we want to write. In line 19 we *load the effective address* of the msg string into the rsi register (lea rsi, [msg]). The *lea* instruction is a different animal from the *mov* instruction. When we say that we want to mov the numeric constant STDOUT into the rsi register, we mean that we want to move the number one (1) into the rdi register. When we say lea rsi, [msg] we mean that we want to move the numeric memory address represented by [msg] into the rsi register. Sometimes you will see something like mov rsi, [listIndex + 8 * rcx]. This behaves just like *load the effective address*. We're loading the address of memory represented by listIndex + 8 * rcx into the rsi register. It's nice of the assembler to take care of the arithmetic for us. It even understands the algebraic precedence of executing multiplication and division before addition and subtraction.

Incidentally, rdi is also known as the destination index register and rsi is also known as the source index register. These two general-purpose registers were originally designed to work with strings, so they are also special-purpose registers. So we are setting the destination to the numeric constant STDOUT and the source to the memory address [msg]. The square brackets around msg indicate that msg is a local variable that can be found in the .data section (or .rodata section) of the program.

The third and final argument is the number of characters that we want to write. In line 20, we move MSGLEN into the rdx register (mov rdx, MSGLEN). Note that the MSGLEN constant was calculated for you by the assembler in line 32. MSGLEN is the current position of the address pointer minus the memory address msg ($-msg).

The syscall (software interrupt) instruction calls the same address no matter what Linux kernel service we want to call. It uses the contents of the rax register to tell it what service we requested. We move the numeric constant, SYS_WRITE (1), into the rax register in line 21.

Once we have our parameters marshaled (moved into the appropriate registers), we pass control to the Linux kernel to perform the service. We do this in line 22 (syscall). The order in which we marshal the arguments doesn't matter. What matters is that when we invoke syscall all of the arguments are available where the kernel service expects to find them. The kernel moves into protected mode and performs the write for you.

Then the kernel goes back into user mode and continues with the next instruction in hello. The next task we want to perform is to tell Linux that our program has finished with the processor and that we want to return control to Linux so that Linux can handle our next request given through the bash shell. It's important to always clean up after yourself.

The syscall in line 22 returns the number of characters actually written in the rax register.

We now want to use the SYS_EXIT Linux kernel *function*. We do this in lines 24 through 27. Linux programs usually return zero to indicate success and a nonzero value to indicate failure. In line 24, we subtract MSGLEN from the number of characters written in rax. If we actually wrote MSGLEN characters, then rax will contain zero; if we didn't, it will contain a nonzero value. We move rax into rdi (the first parameter for SYS_EXIT). Then we set rax to SYS_EXIT and issue the syscall.

What happens to the value you return in the rdi register? SYS_EXIT puts it in rax and it's available to any shell script that might be running your program. The shell can check this value and decide what to, or what not to, do next. You can check your program's return value yourself by typing ***echo $?*** at the shell prompt.

```
js@suse-leap-z4:~/Development/asm_x86_64/hello$ ./hello

Hello, world!

js@suse-leap-z4:~/Development/asm_x86_64/hello$ echo $?
0
```

The sequence of events looks like this. You start off in the shell, which is patiently waiting for you to do something interesting. You type ./hello at the command prompt and Linux looks for hello and finds that it's an executable file on disk in your PWD (./). Linux allocates *RAM* (read-write memory) to your program and loads the program from disk into this allocated memory. It allocates more RAM for a *stack* and sets the CPU's stack pointer register rsp to the top of the stack for your program to use. Linux allocates still more RAM for a heap (a dynamically resizable region of memory associated with memory allocations by your program). It then sets the CPU's instruction pointer register rip to the RAM location associated with the label _start and then commands the CPU to execute the instructions in your program.

Your program uses these *POSIX* functions to write to your own terminal and then to transfer control back to Linux, which puts you back into the shell at the command prompt. As far as you're concerned, it looks like you're the only user on the system. In fact, Linux may be servicing other users, processes (programs), and devices. It is also handling interrupt requests from keyboards, mice, disks, hardware housekeeping timers, and other devices.

Running the DDD Debugger

Now let's run hello in the DDD debugger to see what's happening in every step of the program. But first, make hello in debug mode:

```
js@suse-leap-z4:~/Development/asm_x86_64/hello$ make .debug
```

1. Start DDD by typing the following instruction at the command line.

   ```
   js@suse-leap-z4:~/Development/asm_x86_64/hello$ ddd hello
   ```

You should now see a screen that looks almost like the image in Figure 1-1. Select Status ➤ Registers from DDD's menu and position the Registers window where you can see it easily. Right-click at the beginning of line 18 to set a breakpoint there. Do you see the little stop sign to the left of line 18? That's the symbol for a breakpoint.

Click Run at the top of DDD's Command Tool and your computer screen should look just like the image shown in Figure 1-1.

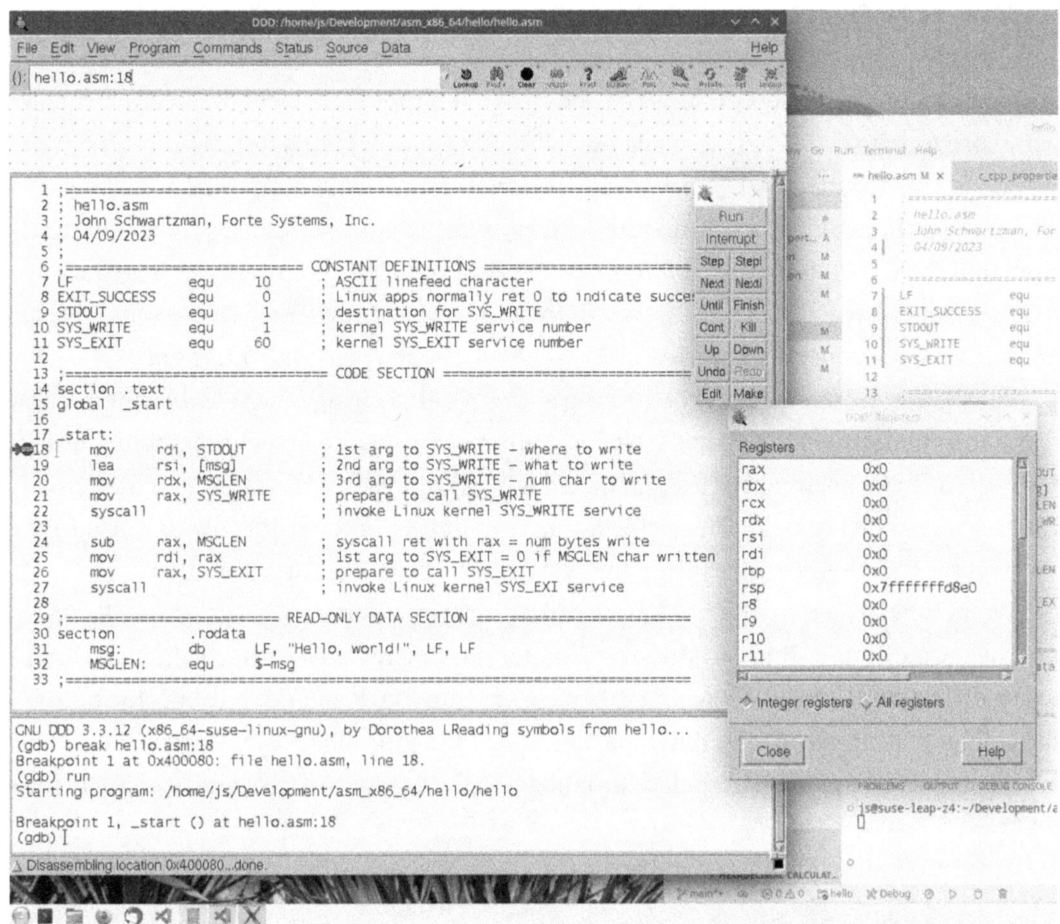

Figure 1-1. *DDD is running hello. It is paused at a breakpoint*

Note the green arrow to the left of line 18. That shows you that DDD is running, but hello is currently paused. When it is next allowed to run, it will execute the instructions beginning at line 18.

Look at the Registers window and note that the value of the rdi register. My rdi currently contains 0x0 (hexadecimal zero). Scroll down in the Registers window so you can see the instruction pointer register. My rip currently contains the 64-bit address 0x400080. That's the RAM address of the first instruction of the program. **The contents of your rip register are likely to be different from mine.**

Now hit the Step button on DDD's Command Tool and notice that the green arrow advances to point to the instruction at line 19. Look at the Registers window again and note that register rdi now contains 0x1. Why? What happened? Well, the first instruction of the program told the CPU to place the value STDOUT, which happens to be decimal 1 (which is also hexadecimal 1), into the rdi register. That's what happened.

Hit Step three more times and notice the changes to the values in rsi, rdx, and rax. Note that the CPU has executed four instructions and loaded four different registers by following the instructions in the first four locations in RAM. (RAM means random-access or read-write memory, as opposed to ROM which means read-only memory.)

Notice that rsi contains the beginning address of the string of bytes we want to write to the terminal (0x4000b4). That's the RAM address where the first character of the string resides. Note the decimal 10 (0x0a in hexadecimal) represents the line feed character, which we're showing as LF. The string appears in line 31 in the read-only data section of the program. **Note the address in your system may be different from mine.**

We're now poised to execute the syscall (or software interrupt) instruction. We've put the correct values into our three parameter passing registers (rdi, rsi, and rdx), and we've put the number of the syscall that we want into rax. We could have performed these four steps in any order. What matters is that the four pieces of information that the syscall needs have been marshaled into the four places where the kernel is going to look for them.

Hit DDD's Step button one more time and you'll see the three lines

```
Hello, World!
```

printed in the bottom window of the three main windows of DDD. If you'd had the execution window open (View ➤ Execution Window), you'd have seen it there, instead.

Hit DDD's Step button three more times and you'll have marshaled the correct information into the single parameter passing register (rdi) and the number of the syscall into rax.

Hit the Step button again and you'll see the hello program finish.

Think, for a moment, about what you've observed. You started a debugger program, which is a visual front end to the gdb debugger. DDD launched gdb, which started our executable program hello. We single-stepped through the hello program and took notice of the changes that occurred to the CPU's registers at each step. We also noted the output of the program in the console.

Activities

1. Define register.
2. Which register keeps track of the memory location of the next instruction to be executed by the CPU?
3. Where and in what order will the BIOS look for the arguments to its various subroutines?
4. What register is used to specify the kernel service we want to invoke?
5. What register is used to return the status of a Linux kernel service to the caller?
6. Modify hello.asm to write a different string. Step through both hello and a.out using DDD. Make sure that you understand what happens at each step of the program.
7. Modify hello.asm to write several sentences.
8. Modify hello.asm so that you invoke the Linux write service several times. Note that just because you wrote a value into a register, it doesn't mean that it will still be there when you need it. Registers are a limited resource, and the BIOS needs to use them to perform its own work.
9. Modify hello.asm so that it prints "Hello, world!" in French. Call your program bonjour.asm.
10. Is printf a *POSIX* function?

CHAPTER 2

Extending BIOS Services

Now that we know how to print, let's print something more interesting. When you have a problem with your computer or with some software and you look online for help, you're often asked to provide information about your environment using Linux's uname command. Of course, you could simply go to a command line interface (CLI) prompt and type uname -a, but that's not much fun.

Our next program, uname.c, is shown in Listing 2-1. Its assembly language equivalent, uname.asm, is shown in Listing 2-2. Listing 2-3 shows the Makefile used to make the two executable programs. These two programs get and print the uname information before returning control to Linux. Build uname.c and uname.asm and satisfy yourself that the two programs produce the same output.

Note A list of the x64 BIOS functions can be found on the internet by searching for Linux System Call Table for x86 64.

Listing 2-1. uname.c

```
// uname.c
// John Schwartzman, Forte Systems, Inc.
// 05/20/2019

#include <stdio.h>           // declaration of printf, perror
#include <stdlib.h>          // defines EXIT_SUCCESS, EXIT_FAILURE
#include <sys/utsname.h>     // declaration of uname, struct utsname

int main(void)
{
    struct utsname buffer;
```


J. Schwartzman, *Assembly Language Reimagined*, https://doi.org/10.1007/979-8-8688-1724-3_2

```

    int retValue = uname(&buffer);

    if (retValue != 0)
    {
        perror("uname");
        return retValue;;
    }

    printf("   OS name:      %s\n", buffer.sysname);
    printf("   node name:    %s\n", buffer.nodename);
    printf("   release:      %s\n", buffer.release);
    printf("   version:      %s\n", buffer.version);
    printf("   machine:      %s\n", buffer.machine);
    return retValue;
}
```

Listing 2-2. uname.asm

```
;========================================================================
; uname.asm - retrieve uname info from the kernel and print it
; John Schwartzman, Forte Systems, Inc.
; 03/31/2023
; linux x86_64
;
;======================= CONSTANT DEFINITIONS ===========================
STDOUT          equ     1           ; file descriptor for terminal
SYS_EXIT        equ    60           ; Linux service ID for SYS_EXIT
SYS_WRITE       equ     1           ; Linux service ID for SYS_WRITE
SYS_UNAME       equ    63           ; Linux service ID for SYS_UNAME
UTSNAME_SIZE    equ    65           ; number of bytes in each *_res entry
LABEL_SIZE      equ    16           ; size of each header
WRITELINE_SIZE  equ     1           ; num bytes to write for linefeed
LF              equ    10           ; ASCII linefeed character

;============================ CODE SECTION ==============================
```

```
section     .text
global      _start                  ; ld expects to find the label _start
_start:                             ; beginning of program
mov rax, SYS_UNAME                  ; prepare to call SYS_UNAME
lea rdi, [sysname_res]              ; rdi points to address of structure
syscall ; call SYS_UNAME to populate .bss data section (uninitialized data)
mov   rdi, rax                      ; if -1 is returned in rax, exit
or    rax, rax                      ; update RFLAGS register
jnz   exit                          ; exit if error getting SYS_UNAME
lea   rsi, [sysname]                ; SYS_WRITE 2nd arg
call  writeLabel                    ; call local method - print w/o linefeed
lea   rsi, [sysname_res]            ; SYS_WRITE 2nd arg
call  writeData                     ; call local method - print with linefeed
lea   rsi, [nodename]               ; print nodename header
call  writeLabel
lea   rsi, [nodename_res]           ; print nodename data
call  writeData
lea   rsi, [release]                ; print release header
call  writeLabel
lea   rsi, [release_res]            ; print release data
call  writeData
lea   rsi, [version]                ; print version header
call  writeLabel
lea   rsi, [version_res]            ; print version data
call  writeData
lea   rsi, [domain]                 ; print domain header
call  writeLabel
lea   rsi, [domain_res]             ; print domain data
call  writeData
```

```

xor   rdi, rdi                    ; rdi = EXIT_SUCCESS (0) - fall into exit

exit:
mov   rax, SYS_EXIT               ; exit program - 1st arg rdi = exit code
syscall                           ; invoke kernel and we're gone

writeLabel:    ;===== local method - caller sets SYS_WRITE 2nd param (rsi) =====
mov   rax, SYS_WRITE              ; Linux service ID
mov   rdi, STDOUT                 ; SYS_WRITE 1st arg
mov   rdx, LABEL_SIZE             ; 4YS_WRITE 3rd arg
syscall                           ; invoke kernel
ret                               ;====== end of writeLabel method =====

writeData:      ;===== local method - caller sets SYS_WRITE 2nd param (rsi) =====
mov   rax, SYS_WRITE              ; Linux service ID
mov   rdi, STDOUT                 ; SYS_WRITE 1st arg
mov   rdx, UTSNAME_SIZE           ; SYS_WRITE 3rd arg
syscall                           ; invoke kernel and fall through to writeNewLine

writeNewLine:                     ;=========== local method ===========
mov   rax, SYS_WRITE              ; Linux service ID
mov   rdi, STDOUT                 ; SYS_WRITE 1st arg
lea   rsi, [linefeed]             ; SYS_WRITE 2nd arg
mov   rdx, WRITELINE_SIZE         ; SYS_WRITE 3rd arg
syscall                           ; invoke kernel
ret                               ; ===== end of writeNeLineMethod =====

;===================== READ-ONLY DATA SECTION ======================
section     .rodata
sysname     db      "   OS name:      "
nodename    db      "   node name:    "
```

```
release     db      "   release:      "
version     db      "   version:      "
domain      db      "   machine:      "
linefeed    db      LF                 ; ASCII linefeed character

;====================== UNINITIALIZED DATA SECTION ===================
section     .bss
sysname_res     resb    UTSNAME_SIZE
nodename_res    resb    UTSNAME_SIZE
release_res     resb    UTSNAME_SIZE
version_res     resb    UTSNAME_SIZE
domain_res      resb    UTSNAME_SIZE
;=====================================================================
```

Listing 2-3. Makefile for uname

```
##########################################################################
#
#        Makefile for uname
#        John Schwartzman, Forte Systems, Inc.
#        12/16/2023
#
#        Commands:  make [.release], make .debug, make clean, make install
#
#        Requires:  ../maketest.sh
#
##########################################################################
PROG  := uname
SHELL := /bin/bash

.release: $(PROG).asm $(PROG).c Makefile
          @source ../maketest.sh && test .release .debug
          yasm -f elf64 -o $(PROG).obj $(PROG).asm  # assemble
          ld $(PROG).obj -o $(PROG)                 # link
          gcc $(PROG).c                             # compile and link a.out

.debug: $(PROG).asm $(PROG).c Makefile
```

```
        @source ../maketest.sh && test .debug .release
        yasm -f elf64 -g dsingle-precision floating pointwarf2 -o $
        (PROG).obj $(PROG).asm   # assemble
        ld -g $(PROG).obj -o $(PROG)   # link
        gcc -g $(PROG).c               # compile and link C version (a.out)

clean:
        rm -f $(PROG) $(PROG).obj a.out .debug .release
##########################################################################

js@suse-leap-z4:~/Development/asm_x86_64/uname$ make release
...
js@suse-leap-z4:~/Development/asm_x86_64/uname$ ./uname
   OS name:      Linux
   node name:    suse-leap-z4
   release:      5.14.21-150400.24.55-default
   version:      #1 SMP PREEMPT_DYNAMIC Mon Mar 27 15:25:48 UTC 2023
                 (cc75cf8)
   machine:      x86_64
js@suse-leap-z4:~/Development/asm_x86_64/uname$ ./a.out
   OS name:      Linux
   node name:    suse-leap-z4
   release:      5.14.21-150400.24.55-default
   version:      #1 SMP PREEMPT_DYNAMIC Mon Mar 27 15:25:48 UTC 2023 (cc75cf8)
   machine:      x86_64
js@suse-leap-z4:~/Development/asm_x86_64/uname$
```

The outputs are the same. Hooray! Before we examine these programs, let's briefly review *Boolean* logic gates and the representation of numbers in the computer.

A Brief Introduction to *Boolean* Logic Gates

A logic gate examines the input levels and produces an output level from them. Take a look at the logic gates shown in Figure 2-1. We see several two-input logic gates followed by their truth tables, their names, and their equations. The truth tables indicate the output, x, for all combinations of inputs, a and b. You'll see examples of logic gates when we discuss uname.asm.

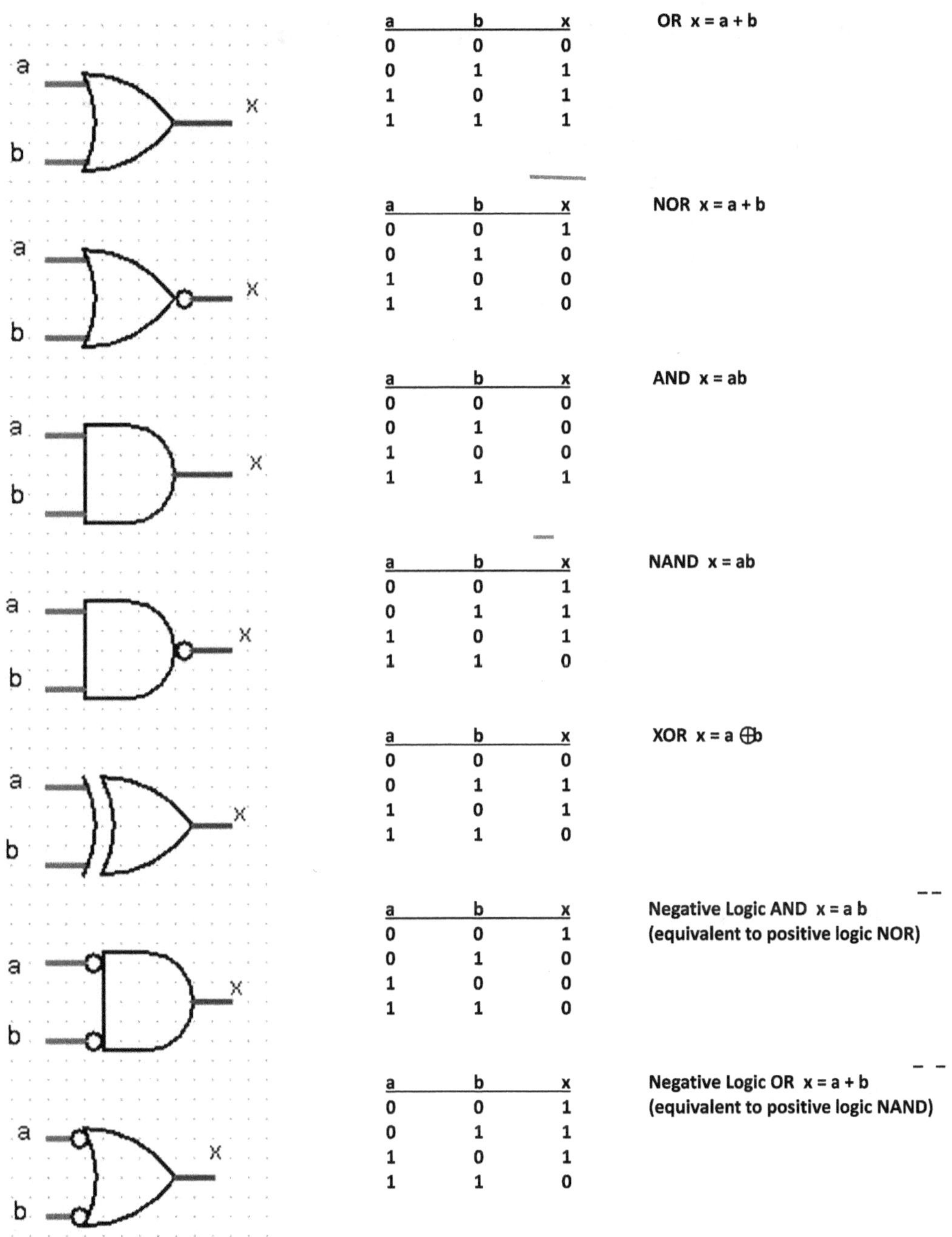

OR $x = a + b$

a	b	x
0	0	0
0	1	1
1	0	1
1	1	1

NOR $x = \overline{a + b}$

a	b	x
0	0	1
0	1	0
1	0	0
1	1	0

AND $x = ab$

a	b	x
0	0	0
0	1	0
1	0	0
1	1	1

NAND $x = \overline{ab}$

a	b	x
0	0	1
0	1	1
1	0	1
1	1	0

XOR $x = a \oplus b$

a	b	x
0	0	0
0	1	1
1	0	1
1	1	0

Negative Logic AND $x = \bar{a}\,\bar{b}$
(equivalent to positive logic NOR)

a	b	x
0	0	1
0	1	0
1	0	0
1	1	0

Negative Logic OR $x = \bar{a} + \bar{b}$
(equivalent to positive logic NAND)

a	b	x
0	0	1
0	1	1
1	0	1
1	1	0

Figure 2-1. *Some two-input logic gates and their truth tables*

Representation of Numbers in the Computer

In a digital computer, we represent all numbers as collections of binary (base 2) values. The computer uses two voltages to represent the two symbols for a binary number. Usually, zero volts (0V) is used to represent a 0 and ~3.3V is used to represent a 1. This keeps things pretty simple. With only two symbols to use, we count up as shown in the base 2 (binary) column. The reason is that components age and their values change over time. That's why we use digital (vs. analog) computers for most computing work.[2]

base 2 (binary)	base 10 (decimal)	base 16 (hexadecimal)
0	0	0
1	1	1
10	2	2
11	3	3
100	4	4
101	5	5
110	6	6
111	7	7
1000	8	8
1001	9	9
1010	10	A
1011	11	B
1100	12	C
1101	13	D
1110	14	E
1111	15	F
10000	16	10
10001	17	11
...	...	...

Memory locations and registers in the CPU are collections of binary digits. The size of a general purpose register in an Intel x86_64 processor is 64 bits. That means we can hold 2^{64} - 1 or *18,446,744,073,709,551,617* (approximately 18 billion billion) different values in a register. Notice how binary maps nicely into hexadecimal. We can represent one nibble (4 bits) of binary with a single hexadecimal digit.

Suppose we have the binary value $0111\ 1000\ 0010\ 1010_2$. We can easily refer to it as $782A_{16}$ in hexadecimal. It's the same value. It's a kind of shorthand.

The CPU contains many 64-input Boolean logic gates, and also 32-input, 16-input, and 8-input logic gates, which go along with the CPU's 32-bit, 16-bit, and 8-bit registers. When we perform an arithmetic or logic operation, certain of these gates save their outputs in the rflags register. For example, when we do a bitwise OR of the value in a register with itself (or rax, rax), then rax doesn't change. So x or x = x or in Boolean algebra we'd say x + x = x. Look at the truth table for the OR gate shown in Figure 2-1. Progressing bit by bit through the register, we can see that 0 + 0 = 0 (zero or zero equals zero) and 1 + 1 = 1 (one or one equals one). So, performing a bitwise OR of a register with itself doesn't change the value of the register, but it does change the values of the rflags register. If rax contains 0 and we perform or rax, rax then we can see that rax will still contain 0 after the OR operation, but bit 6 of the rflags register will be 1. We say that the zero flag ZF = 1. If rax contains 1 and we perform or rax, rax, then rax will still contain 1 after the OR operation, but bit 6 of the rflags register will be 0. We say that ZF = 0.

You can think of this register zero detection logic as a 64-input negative logic AND gate inside the CPU. Only if all 64 binary digits (bits) are 0 then ZF = 1, otherwise ZF = 0. (See Figure 2-1.)

You may be thinking, that's nice, but so what? Well, that's how we programmatically change the order of execution of the program. We can say or rax, rax (or and rax, rax or cmp rax, 0 or sub rax, 0) and then jz next (Jump if Zero to next) where next: is a label somewhere in the program. Or we can say jnz next (Jump if Not Zero to next). You'll see this technique employed in uname.asm.

Table 2-1. *Data Types in the Computer*

Data Type	Size (bits)	Typical Use
byte	8	text character, small integer
word	16	text character, integer
doubleword	32	integer, long integer, long long integer, single-precision floating point
quadword	64	integer, long integer, long long integer, double-precision floating point, memory address
double quadword	128	Integer, packed integers, packed floating points

Be aware that Microsoft uses a doubleword to hold both long integers and long long integers, while Linux uses a quadword to hold the same data types.

Note also that except for characters (which are simply bit patterns), all data types can be signed or unsigned values. Signed integers use the lower half of the data type for the value and the upper half of the data type for the sign. To create a signed number, we do a two's complement operation. A two's complement operation consists of adding 1 to the one's complement of a number. A one's complement simply changes all of the ones to zeros and all of the zeros to ones. For example, the unsigned integer 21 looks like this:

$$\begin{array}{llll} & 0000\ 0000\ 0001\ 0101_2 & = & 16_{10} + 4_{10} + 1_{10} = 21_{10} \\ & 1111\ 1111\ 1110\ 1010_2 & = & \text{one's complement of } 21_{10} \\ +\ 1 & 1111\ 1111\ 1110\ 1011_2 & = & \text{two's complement of } 21_{10} \quad = \quad -21_{10} \end{array}$$

$$\begin{array}{llll} & 0000\ 0000\ 0001\ 0101_2 & = & 21_{10} \\ + & \underline{1111\ 1111\ 1110\ 1011_2} & = & \underline{-21_{10}} \\ & 0000\ 0000\ 0000\ 0000_2 & = & 0_{10} \end{array}$$

From this example, you can see that the sum of 21_{10} + -21_{10} = 0_{10} and we throw away the carry from the most significant bit.

That shows us that subtraction on a computer is the same as two's complement addition. In order to perform a subtraction we add the 1st addend to the two's complement of the 2nd addend. That's what happens automatically when we perform an operation like sub ax, bx. We convert bx to the two's complement of bx and preform add.

There is one further point about numbers in computers, endianness. When multibyte values are placed into memory, how do we determine the value of the number? Intel processors use the *little-endian* format. That is, the least significant byte goes in the lowest memory address and the most significant byte goes in the highest memory address. It's the same when we add bytes to multibyte registers and data types: the least significant byte goes into the lowest address and the most significant byte goes into the highest memory address.

The program uname.c should not present any challenges. We declare a utsname structure and give it the name buffer in line 11. In line 13, we invoke the glibc uname function to fill the buffer structure. After that, we simply print the information that glibc has previously placed inside the buffer structure.

Now let's look at uname.asm. The program begins at the _start label in line 21. The first thing we're going to do is to invoke the SYS_UNAME Linux kernel service. But, before we do this, we must put the correct value into our first and only parameter passing register (rdi) and the number of the syscall that we want into rax.

We invoke SYS_UNAME with the syscall in line 24. That populates the uninitiated data section of our address space (lines 90–96). Once that is done, we check for success by examining the rax register after executing syscall. If it's nonzero, we need to exit because the syscall failed (presumably with a one). If it's zero, we can print a label, print the corresponding field in the uninitialized data section, and print a line-feed character. We do this five times and the program ends.

We now need to look closely at how we determine success or failure. In line 26, we move the value returned by the SYS_UNAME Linux kernel service into rdi. We need to determine whether rax is equal to zero. In order to find out, we need to perform an arithmetic or Boolean logic operation on rax. We chose to do the Boolean logic operation or rax, rax in line 27. This performs a 64-bit bit-wise OR operation on rax with itself. This leaves rax alone, but sets the flags register.

The DDD Debugger

Let's run uname in the DDD debugger. But first, change the working directory to ~/Development/asm_x86_64/uname and make uname in debug mode.

```
js@suse-leap-z4:~/Development/asm_x86_64/hello$ cd ../uname
js@suse-leap-z4:~/Development/asm_x86_64/uname$ make .debug
```

Now start DDD by typing the following instruction:

```
js@suse-leap-z4:~/Development/asm_x86_64/uname$ ddd uname
```

You should now see a screen that looks almost like the image in Figure 2-2. First Select Status ➤ Registers from DDD's menu and position the Registers window where you can see it easily. Then right-click at the beginning of line 28 to set a breakpoint there. Now Click Run at the top of DDD's Command Tool and your computer screen should look just like the image shown in Figure 2-2.

We've just executed the SYS_UNAME syscall and the result, which is returned in rax, is zero. That means SYS_UNAME succeeded. Verify this by examining the rax register. Also, take a look at the rflags register, which in DDD is labeled eflags. My rflags says IF, which means Interrupt Flags enabled. Note that rdi and rax both have the same value. We copied rax to rdi in line 26 just in case we take the jump to exit in line 28. rdi is the first and only parameter to SYS_EXIT which is invoked at the exit label.

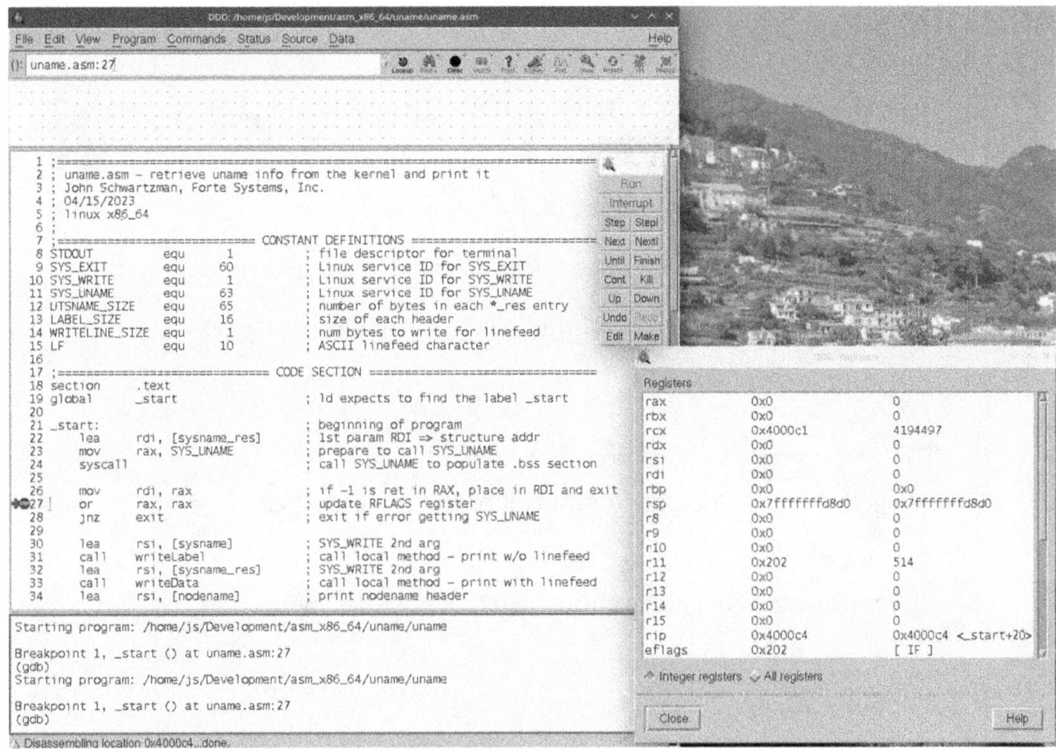

***Figure 2-2.** DDD is sitting at a breakpoint at line 27 of uname.asm*

Press the Step key to execute line 27. Examine the rax register and the rflags register. The rax register should still contain 0, which makes sense since we decided that OR-ing a register with itself should not change its value. rflags should have changed, however. My rflags shows PF (Parity Flag), IF (Interrupt Flag), and ZF (Zero Flag). ZF means the zero flag is set. What is going to happen at the next step? Will we jump or not? If you said no, you are correct. The instruction jnz exit means Jump if Not Zero to the exit label.

Press the Step button and notice that the green arrow (rip) is pointing to line 30. We did not jump to line 57 (the first instruction following the exit label). SYS_UNAME reported success, and now we're going to execute several calls to writeLabel and writeData methods. You might care to step into these methods.

Note that writeNewLine is an alternate entrance to the writeData method. It's never called in the code, but if we desired we could use it to print an empty line wherever we wanted an empty line.

Press Cont (continue) when you're ready to execute the program to the next breakpoint or to the end or the program if you have not set any more breakpoints.

Activities

1. Draw the truth table for a three-input AND gate with inputs a, b, and c, and output x.
2. Draw the truth table for a three-input OR gate.
3. Draw the truth table for a three-input negative logic AND gate.
4. Draw the symbol for a single-input NOT gate and its truth table.
5. $0101\ 1100\ 1010\ 0000_2 = \_\_\_\_\_\_\_\_\_\_\_\_\_\_\_\__{16}$.
6. $0FA01_{16} = \_\_\_\_\_\_\_\_\_\_\_\_\_\_\_\_\_\_\_\_\_\_\_\__2$.
7. A negative logic AND gate is equivalent to a positive logic ________ gate.
8. A negative logic OR gate is equivalent to a positive logic _________ gate.
9. A doubleword contains ________ bytes.
10. A double quadword can hold _______ packed integers.
11. What data type do we use to hold a memory address?
12. What is the 16-bit two's complement of 39_{10}?
13. Demonstrate $x = 39_{10} - 21_{10}$ by performing two's complement addition. What is the value of x?
14. Write Activity 13 as a CPU instruction.

CHAPTER 3

Prefer glibc over BIOS Calls, uname Reprise

In this chapter, we are going to abandon the Linux kernel services and use the glibc, the *GNU* C run-time library, instead of calling the Linux kernel services directly. The glibc functions are, in many cases, thin wrappers around the Linux kernel services and the preferred way to access Linux kernel services. Before we begin examining code, though, we need to briefly mention the stack and the C Calling Convention.

The Stack

The stack is a new allocation of memory that Linux provides to each running program. It is like a stack of plates on a spring-loaded platform in a cafeteria. When a plate is removed from the stack, the spring forces a new plate into the top position; when you add a plate to the stack, all the other plates are pushed down and the new plate is the one on top.

On an Intel x86_64, the stack grows downward in memory. There is a stack pointer register, rsp, that points to the current stack position. When we PUSH a value onto the stack, rsp is automatically decremented by the size of the push (eight bytes), and the value being pushed is written to the memory now pointed to by rsp. When we POP a value from the stack, rsp is automatically incremented by eight bytes and the value in memory pointed to by rsp is returned. The stack is a last-in first-out (LIFO) data structure in memory.

J. Schwartzman, *Assembly Language Reimagined*, https://doi.org/10.1007/979-8-8688-1724-3_3

We can use the stack as temporary storage:

```
push    rdi                 ; temporarily save rdi in stack
; do something with rdi that changes its value
xor     rdi, rdi            ; rdi = 0
pop     rdi                 ; restore prev value of rdi from stack
```

We can also use the stack to swap two registers:

```
; swap rcx and rdx
push   rcx                  ; save rcx
mov    rcx, rdx             ; rcx ← rdx
pop    rdx                  ; restore rdx (formerly rcx)
```

The stack is also used to keep track of return addresses. When we issue the call instruction to access a function or method, the program address of the instruction following the call instruction is automatically pushed onto the stack. This is the return address. When our function or method encounters a ret (return) op code, the return address is retrieved from the stack and placed in the instruction pointer register, rip. That means that whenever you call a method or function, which are both subroutines, you can always continue exactly where you left off after the subroutine finishes.

The stack is also a place to store local variables. Local variables are also known as automatic variables. We will encounter local variables in cmdline.asm (Chapter 4).

As we shall soon see, the stack can also be used to pass arguments to functions and methods.

Intel tells us that the stack needs a little care and attention. Intel expects the stack pointer register (rsp) to be maintained on sixteen byte boundaries in memory. That means that the hexadecimal value for rsp should end in 0. So, what do we have to do? Place the following instructions (shown in bold type) at the beginning and end of your main function and in every non-leaf function in your program (a leaf function doesn't call any functions and it doesn't use the stack, except to find its return address):

```
VAR_SIZE        equu    8           ; each local var is 8 bytes
NUM_VAR         equ     4           ; number local var (round up to
                                      even num)

functionName:
    push    rbp
```

```
mov     rbp, rsp
sub     rsp, NUM_VAR * VAR_SIZE ; make space for local var (if needed)

; body of functionName
; ...

leave                           ; Set rsp to RBP, then pop RBP
ret                             ; return from functionName with
                                ; retCode in rax
```

The C Calling Convention

The Intel x86_64 CPU has a limited number of registers. In order for Linux, C/C++ and assembly language programs to play together nicely, we need to know which registers our assembly language programs may change and which must be preserved. We need to know which registers may be changed by the methods we call and which will be preserved. We need to know which registers are used to pass arguments to our methods, and our methods need to know where to find their parameters. Our assembly language programs can only work properly if we obey the same rules that Linux and glibc obey.

The six argument passing registers are, in order: rdi, rsi, rdx, rcx, r8, and r9. (This is almost the same as for Linux kernel services, except that rcx is substituted for r10.) So, if we're calling a glibc method, we pass the first argument in rdi, the second in rsi, the third in rdx, the fourth in rcx, the fifth in r8, and the sixth in r9. Of course, if a glibc method only takes three arguments, then we only have to worry about marshaling arguments into rdi, rsi, and rdx.

Linux kernel services are limited to a maximum of six arguments, but that's not enough for glibc. If a glibc function takes more than six arguments, we pass the first six arguments normally (in the six argument passing registers), but any additional arguments are pushed onto the stack. The callee will get its parameters from the six argument passing registers, and then it will access the remaining parameters from the stack. The caller is responsible for removing them from the stack. We'll see an example of this in Chapter 5.

These rules are set forth in the System 5 Application Binary Interface (ABI) of the AMD64 Architecture Processor Supplement.[2] You know all about the Application Programming Interface (API).[3] An API is a software contract between two or more pieces of software, which describes how the pieces of software communicate with each other. The ABI defines the low-level binary interface between two or more pieces of software on a particular architecture. It describes how an application interacts with itself, interacts with the kernel, and interacts with libraries. Table 3-1 specifies who is responsible for saving and restoring registers.

Table 3-1. *Register Usage*

Register	Usage
rax	Return Value – Caller Saved if needed
rbx	Callee Saved – you don't need to preserve it
rcx	4th Argument – Caller Saved if needed
rdx	3rd Argument – Caller Saved if needed
rsi	2nd Argument – Caller Saved if needed
rdi	1st Argument – Caller Saved if needed
rbp	Base Pointer – Callee Saved
rsp	Stack Pointer
r8	5th Argument – Caller Saved if needed
r9	6th Argument – Caller Saved if needed
r10	Temporary Register – Caller Saved if needed
r11	Temporary Register – Caller Saved if needed
r12	Callee Saved
r13	Callee Saved
r14	Callee Saved
r15	Callee Saved

The Linker

The gcc linker understands all about linking with the GNU glibc standard C library. It uses the gnu linker ld to do its work, but it does a lot in the background before invoking ld. There are glibc startup and shutdown code modules that must be linked to the executable image of your program.

The glibc code contains the label _start inside itself. The glibc code at _start does some initialization, calls your main() function, and waits for it to return. It then does some cleanup and issues the SYS_EXIT syscall. Whatever is left in rax when your main() returns is moved into rdi before the SYS_EXIT kernel service is invoked. What we did in the Chapters 1 and 2 is handled automatically by glibc. In future, exiting from main() will automatically return control to Linux.

The long and short of it is that when your assembly language programs use glibc, they must link with gcc rather than ld (gcc calls ld for us). All of the remaining Makefile listings use gcc to link assembly language modules.

We have rewritten uname.asm to use glibc. It incorporates the rules described above. This program is called uname2.asm (See Listing 3-1) and it is much more elegant that uname.asm. Listing 3-2 shows a Bash script we will us to print the output of the program. Listing 3-3 shows the Bash script install.sh and Listing 3-4 shows the makefile for uname2.asm.

Listing 3-1. uname2.asm

```
;==========================================================================
; uname2.asm - retrieve uname info from glibc and print it
; John Schwartzman, Forte Systems, Inc.
; 05/20/2023
; linux x86_64
;
;======================== CONSTANT DEFINITIONS ======================
UTSNAME_SIZE       equ     65         ; number of bytes in each *_res entry
LF                 equ     10         ; ASCII linefeed character
EOL                equ      0         ; end of line

;========================== CODE SECTION ============================
section    .text
global     main                       ; gcc expects to find the label main
extern     uname, printf              ; tell yasm and linker about external functions

main:                                 ; beginning of program
      push  rbp                       ; set up stack frame
```

```
        mov   rbp, rsp                    ; set up stack frame - stack is aligned

        lea   rdi, [sysname_res]          ; 1st param rdi => structure addr
        call  uname                       ; invoke glibc function uname
        or    rax, rax                    ; was uname successful?
        jnz   exit                        ;   jump if no
                                          ; marshal arguments for printf
        lea   rdi, [unameFmtStr]          ; 1st arg to printf - format string
        lea   rsi, [sysname_res]          ; 2nd arg to printf - 1st placeholder
        lea   rdx, [nodename_res]         ; 3rd arg to printf - 2nd placeholder
        lea   rcx, [release_res]          ; 4th arg to printf - 3rd placeholder
        lea   r8,  [version_res]          ; 5th arg to printf - 4th placeholder
        lea   r9,  [machine_res]          ; 6th arg to printf - 5th placeholder
        xor   eax, eax                    ; no floating point args for printf
        call  printf                      ; invoke glibc function printf

        xor   rax, rax                    ; return EXIT_SUCCESS (0)

exit:
        leave                             ; undo 1st 2 instructions - restore rsp
        ret                               ; this returns control to Linux

;====================== READ-ONLY DATA SECTION =======================
section      .rodata
unameFmtStr  db    "   OS name:      %s", LF,
             db    "   node name:    %s", LF,
             db    "   release:      %s", LF,
```

```
            db    "   version:     %s", LF,
            db    "   machine:     %s", LF, EOL ; NOTE: str is 1 ASCIIZ str

;====================== UNINITIALIZED DATA SECTION ===================
section     .bss
sysname_res   resb    UTSNAME_SIZE    ; .bss contains struct utsname
nodename_res  resb    UTSNAME_SIZE
release_res   resb    UTSNAME_SIZE
version_res   resb    UTSNAME_SIZE
machine_res   resb    UTSNAME_SIZE
;=====================================================================
```

Listing 3-2. The os-distro.sh Shell Script

```
#!/bin/bash
##########################################################################
# os-distro.sh - utility shell script to display uname and distro information
# John Schwartzman
# 05/20/2023
# Forte Systems, Inc.
##########################################################################
printf "\nDATE:\n " # print 1st title
/usr/bin/date | sed -n 'P' # display date up to newline
printf "OS:\n" # print 2nd title
/usr/local/bin/uname2 # invoke uname2
printf "DISTRO:\n " # print 3rd title
cat /etc/os-release | \
sed -n 's/.*PRETTY_NAME=\"/PRETTY_NAME: /p' | sed -n 's/\"//p'
printf " "
cat /etc/os-release | \
sed -n 's/.*VERSION=\"/VERSION: /p' | sed -n 's/\"//p'
printf "\n" # print blank line
```

Listing 3-3. install.sh

```
#!/bin/bash
##############################################################################
# install.sh - utility shell script to copy uname2 and os-distro.sh
#              to /usr/local/bin
#      John Schwartzman, Forte Systems, Inc.
#      12/17/2023
##############################################################################
sudo cp uname2 /usr/local/bin/
sudo cp os-distro.sh /usr/local/bin/os-distro
```

Listing 3-4. Makefile for uname2

```
##############################################################################
#
#      Makefile for uname
#      John Schwartzman, Forte Systems, Inc.
#      12/16/2023
#
#      Commands:  make [release], make debug, make clean
#   Requires:  ../asm/maketest.sh
#
##############################################################################
PROG  := uname
SHELL := /bin/bash

.release: $(PROG).asm $(PROG).c Makefile
      @source ../maketest.sh && test .release .debug
      yasm -f elf64 -o $(PROG).obj $(PROG).asm          # assemble
      ld $(PROG).obj -o $(PROG)                         # link
      gcc $(PROG).c                                     # compile and
                                                          link a.out

.debug: $(PROG).asm $(PROG).c Makefile
      @source ../maketest.sh && test .debug .release
      yasm -f elf64 -g dwarf2 -o $(PROG).obj $(PROG).asm # assemble
```

```
	ld -g $(PROG).obj -o $(PROG)                        # link
	gcc -g $(PROG).c                                    # compile and
	                                                      link a.out

clean:
	rm -f $(PROG) $(PROG).obj a.out .debug .release
############################################################################
```

Notice that Makefile no longer calls ld directly. It calls gcc to perform linking; gcc will call ld to perform loading.

Data Sections

What's with all the data sections in our program? We have section .data, section .rodata, and section .bss. Section .bss contains allocations that do not have any data attached. This section reduces the size of the executable because it is not initialized until runtime. At runtime, it is initialized by the loader utility, ld. Section .data contains normal read/write initialized data and is included in the size of the executable. Section .rodata is read-only memory. It contributes to the size of the executable, but will not allow the programmer to change the data. It provides protection against programmer error.

The uname2.asm Program

The first thing we do in our main function is to add the boilerplate code to manage the stack. Then we marshal our single argument for uname, which is the address of the structure to hold the uname information. Then we invoke the glibc function uname and check the result (or rax, rax in line 23). If rax contains a nonzero number, then we return to the glibc startup code with the failure code in rax.

Note that unameFmtStr (line 43) is a single ASCIIZ string with five string placeholders. We'll be able to print it with one call to printf. In lines 26–31 we marshal the arguments for printf. In line 32, we zero eax (the lower half or 32 bits of rax). The glibc function printf is complicated. It needs eax set to zero to tell it that there are no floating point arguments in its format string.

We invoke glibc's printf function in line 33. We assume that printf was successful and zero rax to indicate success.

Finally, we execute the required boilerplate code to restore rbp and rsp, and we're done. The glibc startup code then moves rax into rdi and invokes the SYS_EXIT Linux kernel service code to return control to Linux.

The os-distro.sh Shell Script

The program uname.asm does just what it's supposed to do, but it seems a shame to stop there.

A description of the operating system is nice, but it would be more useful if we added a description of the Linux *distro* (distribution). The distro details are located in the file /etc/os-release. This version is from Ubuntu. You can type the following command to see your own distro's version:

```
js@ubuntu-z4:~$ cat /etc/os-release
PRETTY_NAME="Ubuntu 22.04.2 LTS"
NAME="Ubuntu"
VERSION_ID="22.04"
VERSION="22.04.2 LTS (Jammy Jellyfish)"
VERSION_CODENAME=jammy
ID=ubuntu
ID_LIKE=debian
HOME_URL="https://www.ubuntu.com/"
SUPPORT_URL="https://help.ubuntu.com/"
BUG_REPORT_URL="https://bugs.launchpad.net/ubuntu/"
PRIVACY_POLICY_URL="https://www.ubuntu.com/legal/terms-and-policies/
privacy-policy"
UBUNTU_CODENAME=jammy
js@ubuntu-z4:~$
```

We'd like to extract the PRETTY_NAME and the VERSION fields from this file and print them following the uname info, and we do it using the bash script file, os-distro.sh (See listing 3-3). This is not assembly language, but shell scripts are used everywhere in Linux and so we now demonstrate a small bash shell script. Our script relies on the stream editor sed to manipulate some strings.

Executing os-distro.sh on a Ubuntu distribution yields the result shown below.

```
js@ubuntu-z4:~$ os-distro

DATE:
   Sat May 20 07:14:28 PM EDT 2023
OS:
   OS name:     Linux
   node name:   ubuntu-z4
   release:     5.19.0-41-generic
   version:     #42~22.04.1-Ubuntu SMP PREEMPT_DYNAMIC Tue Apr 18
                17:40:00 UTC 2
   machine:     x86_64
DISTRO:
   PRETTY_NAME: Ubuntu 22.04.2 LTS
   VERSION:     22.04.2 LTS (Jammy Jellyfish)
```

How did we get this display? The working of os-distro.sh is shown in Table 3-2.

Table 3-2. *A Line by Line Description of os-distro.sh*

Line(s)	Purpose
1	Comment line #!/bin/bash tells script that it needs to run under bash shell.
2 – 7	Comment lines.
8	Print first title.
9	Display date up to newline
10	Print second title.
11	Invoke uname2
12	Print third title

(*continued*)

Table 3-2. (*continued*)

Line(s)	Purpose
13 – 14	Pipe output of cat /etc/os-release into sed and search for a string zero or more characters long that begins with any character and ends with "PRETTY_NAME=", and replace it with "PRETTY_NAME: " followed by the rest of the string found. Pipe this string into sed and search for a quote character. Replace the quote character with nothing followed by the rest of the string found.
15	Print three spaces.
16 – 17	Repeat lines 13 and 14 except search for "VERSION=", and replace it with "VERSION:
18	Print a blank line.

You may type **make install** to compile and link the release version of uname.asm and execute install.sh. The script install.sh uses sudo to copy files into the restricted directory /usr/local/bin. Sudo is used to request administrative privilege from Linux. If your user id is in the sudoers list and you're requesting a privilege that has been granted to you, then make install will succeed. If your id is not in the sudoers list, you will be allowed to proceed with a warning. All sudo operations are logged by Linux.

Activities

1. What boilerplate code must you add to every assembly language program that uses glibc?
2. What linker must you invoke for every assembly language program that uses glibc?
3. Why did we replace _start with main when we started using glibc?
4. Rewrite our first program, hello.asm (Listing 1-2), to use glibc instead of the Linux kernel services. Take a look at Listing 1-1: hello.c. This is what you want to convert into assembly language. Remember to link and load using gcc rather than ld.

5. Write the program readFile.asm to read and print the contents of the file /etc/os-release. You will need to use the glibc functions fopen, fgets, fclose, and printf. Add these component functions to macro.inc. Add building readFile as a task to Makefile.

6. Why do we copy uname2 and os-distro to /usr/local/bin?

7. Modify Makefile so that 'make install' doesn't invoke ./install.sh, but does the work itself.

8. Add the aliases mr, md, mc, and mi to your bash ~/.alias file in order to make it easier to build.

```
alias mr='make release'
alias md='make debug'
alias mc='make clean'
alias mi='make install'
```

9. Why do we prefer glibc over direct calls to the BIOS?

CHAPTER 4

Passing Information to a Program on the Command Line

Programs often need data to do their work. We can read data from a file, from the keyboard, and from the program itself. (Programs can have data embedded in the code. We call that data immediate operands. For example, in the instruction **mov rax, 23**, mov is the op code, and rax is operand, and 23 is the immediate operand.) Another very easy way for a program to get small amounts of data is to place it on the command line when we execute a program. We'll use that method in cmdline.c and cmdline.asm.

Listing 4-1. cmdline.c

```
// cmdline.c
// John Schwartzman, Forte Systems, Inc.
// 04/25/2023

#include <stdio.h>                              // declares printf
#include <stdlib.h>                             // defines EXIT_SUCCESS

int main(int argc, char* argv[])
{
    printf("\n");                               // print blank line
    printf("argc    =  %d\n", argc);            // print argc
    for (int i = 0; i < argc; i++)
```


J. Schwartzman, *Assembly Language Reimagined*, https://doi.org/10.1007/979-8-8688-1724-3_4

```
    {
        printf("argv[%d] = %s\n", i, argv[i]);    // print argv[i]
    }
printf("\n");                                     // print blank line
return EXIT_SUCCESS;
}
```

Listing 4-2. cmdline.asm

```
;==============================================================================
; cmdline.asm - retrieve cmdline info from the OS and print it
; John Schwartzman, Forte Systems, Inc.
; 04/26/2023
; linux x86_64
;
;========================= CONSTANT DEFINITIONS =======================
LF          equ     10                         ; ASCII linefeed char
EO          equ      0                         ; end of line
TAB         equ      9                         ; ASCII tab char
ARG_SIZE    equ      8                         ; size of argv vector & size of a push
VAR_SIZE    equ      8                         ; each local var is 8 bytes
NUM_VAR     equ      4                         ; number local var (round up to even num)

;======================= DEFINE LOCAL VARIABLES =======================
%define     index   qword [rsp + VAR_SIZE * (NUM_VAR - 4)]    ; rsp +  0
%define     argc    qword [rsp + VAR_SIZE * (NUM_VAR - 3)]    ; rsp +  8
%define     argv0   qword [rsp + VAR_SIZE * (NUM_VAR - 2)]    ; rsp + 16

;=========================== CODE SECTION =============================
section     .text
global      main                               ; gcc linker expects main, not _start
```

```
extern      printf                           ; tell assembler/linker about externals
main:                                        ; program starts here
    push    rbp                              ; method prefix - set up stack frame
    mov     rbp, rsp                         ; method prefix - set up stack frame
    sub     rsp, NUM_VAR * VAR_SIZE          ; make space for local variables
    xor     rax, rax                         ; initialize local variables
    mov     index, rax                       ; index = 0
    mov     argc, rdi                        ; argc  = rdi (1st arg to main)
    mov     argv0, rsi                       ; argv0 = rsi (2nd arg to main)
    lea     rdi, [formatc]                   ; 1st arg to printf - formatc string
    mov     rsi, argc                        ; 2nd arg to printf - argc
    call    print                            ; printf argc
argvLoop:                                    ; print each argv[i] - do-while loop
    lea     rdi, [formatv]                   ; 1st arg to printf - formatv string
    mov     rsi, index                       ; 2nd arg to printf - index
    mov     rax, argv0
    mov     rdx, [rax + rsi * ARG_SIZE]      ; 3rd arg to printf - rdx => argv[i]
    call    print                            ; print argv[i]
```

```

        inc     index                           ; index++
        mov     rax, index
        cmp     rax, argc                       ; index == argc?
        jl      argvLoop                        ; jump if no - print more argv[]

        call    printNewLine
        xor     eax, eax                        ; eax = EXIT_SUCCESS - fall through to finish

finish:                                         ; ==== this is the end of the program ===
        leave                                   ; method suffix - undo 1st 2 instr in main
        ret                                     ; method suffix - return with retCode in rax

;========================== LOCAL METHODS ==========================
printNewLine:                                   ; local method (alt entry to print)
        lea     rdi, [newLine]                  ; init only arg and fall through to print

print:                                          ; rdi, rsi and rdx are args to printf
        push    rbp                             ; method prefix - set up stack frame
        mov     rbp, rsp                        ; method prefix - set up stack frame

        xor     eax, eax                        ; no floating point args to printf
        call    printf

```

```
69      leave                                   ; method suffix - undo
                                                  1st 2 inst of print
70      ret                                     ; method suffix - return
71
72 ;====================== READ-ONLY DATA SECTION =====================
73 section      .rodata
74 formatc      db      LF, "argc    = %d",  LF, EOL
75 formatv      db      "argv[%d] = %s", LF, EOL
76 newLine      db      LF, EOL
77 ;===================================================================
```

The program cmdline.c should be easy to understand. We can see that the function int main(int argc, char* argv[]) takes two arguments, argc and argv. The argument argc is an integer that tells main how many arguments there are on the command line. The argument argv is an array of character pointers. Another way to say that is that argv is an array of the addresses of the strings passed to the program. The argument argv[0] points to the program path, argv[1] points to the first argument, argv[2] points to the second argument, and so on.

How would you expect Linux to pass the arguments to a program's main function? If you said "using the command passing registers," you'd be correct. The rdi register contains the integer argc and rsi contains the address of argv[0]. Whether Linux is invoking a C program or an assembly language program, or any other type of program, it always passes the arguments in the same way.

You'll notice that cmdline.c doesn't have any mention of registers. That is abstracted away by the C programming language! The program cmdline.c has the variables argc and argv, and you now know how they get populated behind the scenes.

The program prints a blank line, then a line containing the value of argc. It then enters a for-loop. We have a local variable, i, which is declared and initialized to zero at the beginning of the for-loop. For each value of i from 0 to argc, we print the contents of argv[i]. Then we print a blank line and return EXIT_SUCCESS (0) to Linux.

We'll now take a look at cmdline.asm. We start with some constant definitions in lines 7–13. Some programmers don't bother with constant definitions; they just sprinkle the constant values into the code. We feel that's a bad approach. Those numbers, sprinkled through the code may not mean anything to the poor soul looking at the code.

They appear to be "magic" numbers. Assembly language is hard to read; it contains all the details of everything the CPU is doing. The readers of the code deserve all the help they can get. We encourage you to use constant definitions and lots and lots of comments in your assembly code!

In lines 15–18, we define our local variables. Note that they are *quad words (eight bytes or 64 bits)*. Each local variable is defined by its position in the stack frame. We have index at rsp, argc at rsp + 8, and argv0 at rsp + 16. If these variables are on the stack, how do we keep them from interfering with the other functions of the stack? Simple, we use the instruction sub rsp, NUM_VAR * VAR_SIZE. This subtraction moves rsp below our local variables. Remember that the stack grows downward; that's why we subtract. So the top of the stack is at a position past our local variables; and the stack pointer, rsp, decrements and increments without disturbing our local variables.

In line 22, we tell the linker where to find our main method. There must be exactly one globally accessible main() in a program; if there are two or more modules in a program, only one module may have a main.

In line 23, we tell the linker that we're going to use the glibc function printf().

Finally, main begins with the two instruction method prologue as discussed above. It then makes space for four local variables. We're only using three local variables, but we always round up to an even number so that the stack will be properly aligned.

We then populate our local variables. Our loop variable, index, is initialized to zero. The variables argc and argv0 are populated from the first two argument passing registers.

We then marshal our arguments and call our local function print, which zeroes rax and passes on the arguments to printf. The method printf() uses *varadic* argument handling, which simply means that it can be called with a variable number of arguments. The prototype of printf is int printf(char* format, ...).

The first time we call print() (line 37) the ASCIIZ format string is LF, "argc = %d", LF, EOL (line 74). The printf method uses the format string to determine how many arguments it is being passed. There must be at least one argument, the format string, the address of which is passed in the rdi register. Looking at the format string, we see that it contains one %d, which is a placeholder for an integer. So after printf digests the format string, it sees that it needs one more argument, an integer, which it looks for at the address contained in the rsi register.

The printf function assumes that all the arguments have been marshaled before the method is entered.

Note that print has an alternate entry point, printNewLine. printNewLine sets the rdi register, which is the only argument to printf that's needed in this case.

We then enter a while loop that starts with index = 0 and continues while index < argc. For each value of index, we print the format string "argv[%d] = %s", LF, EOL. Note that rdi points to the format string (formatv) and rsi contains the index (%d). %s is a string placeholder, and it is pointed to by rdx. You may be confused by the multiplication and addition that we use to populate rdx (line 43). We want the string that is pointed to by argv0, the string that is pointed to by argv0 + 8, the string that is pointed to by argv0 + 16, etc. Why? Well, argv0, which is argv[0], points to our first string in the argv array. A string pointer is 64-bits, which is also 8-bytes. The first 8-bytes of argv0 taken together constitute the pointer to argv[0]. The second 8-bytes of argv0 taken together constitute the pointer to argv[1], etc.

Here is the loop again:

```
39 argvLoop:                                   ; print each argv[i] - do-while loop
40     lea rdi, [formatv]                      ; 1st arg to printf - formatv string
41         mov      rsi, index                 ; 2nd arg to printf - index
42         mov      rax, argv0
43         mov      rdx, [rax + rsi * ARG_SIZE] ; 3rd arg to printf - rdx => argv[i]
44         call     print                      ; print argv[i] (print is a macro)
45
46         inc      index                      ; index++
47         mov      rax, index
48         cmp      rax, argc                  ; index == argc?
49         jl       argvLoop                   ; jump if no - print more argv[]
```

Lines 40 and 41 marshal rdi (formatv) and rsi (index). In line 42, rax points to the beginning of the argv[] array. Then in line 43, rdx = argv0 + index * 8, and we're ready to print.

For each iteration of the loop, we increment index (line 46). We then compare index to argc (lines 47–48). Compare is a subtraction (index - argc) that doesn't save the result. After the signed number comparison, we check the rflags register (the sign flag (SF) and the overflow flag (OF)). If index is less than argc, we jump to the beginning of the loop and perform another iteration. Run cmdline in the debugger and set a breakpoint at line 49 and verify that the program behaves as you expect. Satisfy yourself that the loop in cmdline.c is functionally equivalent to the loop in cmdline.asm. Figure 4-1 was created by issuing the command "ddd --args cmdline a b c d goldfish" and setting a breakpoint at the end of the loop. Incidentally, numbers on the command line are really strings containing ASCII digit characters. Glibc has functions like atoi(), atol(), and atof() to convert such strings to numbers.

Now run cmdline with the command line argument "*.*". The output looks like this:

```
suse-tw-z4@~/Development/asm_x86_64/cmdline$ ./cmdline *.*

argc    = 10
argv[0] = ./cmdline
argv[1] = a.out
argv[2] = cmdline.asm
argv[3] = cmdline.c
argv[4] = cmdline.obj
argv[5] = printEnvVar2.asm
argv[6] = printEnvVar2.obj
argv[7] = printEnvVar.asm
argv[8] = printEnvVar.c
argv[9] = printEnvVar.obj
```

Surprised? The Linux shell, bash, looks at the current working directory, CWD, and returns its contents by matching the wildcard expression "*.*". In this case, one command line argument returns nine matching files. Bash even sorts the returned values into alphabetical order for you.

The string "*.*" is called a regular expression, and it will match all of the file names that have two strings of any sizes separated by a period. Here are some of the properties of regular expressions:

<table>
<tr><th colspan="3">Summary of Regular Expressions</th></tr>
<tr><td>Wildcard</td><td>.</td><td>Matches any character (‘.’ matches a period in file matching)</td></tr>
<tr><td></td><td>*</td><td>Matches any string (but not a period in file matching)</td></tr>
<tr><td>Quantification</td><td>?</td><td>Zero or one occurrence of the preceding element</td></tr>
<tr><td></td><td>*</td><td>Zero or more occurrences of preceding element</td></tr>
<tr><td></td><td>+</td><td>One or more occurrence of the preceding element</td></tr>
<tr><td></td><td>{n}</td><td>Exactly n occurrences of the preceding element</td></tr>
<tr><td></td><td>{min,}</td><td>Proceeding element is matched min or more times</td></tr>
<tr><td></td><td>{,max}</td><td>Proceeding element is matched up to max times</td></tr>
<tr><td></td><td>{min,
max}</td><td>Proceeding element is matched up to min times, but not more than max times</td></tr>
<tr><td>Boolean OR</td><td>|</td><td>Matches element one OR element two
gr(a|e)y matches gray or grey (USA or UK spellings)</td></tr>
<tr><td>Grouping</td><td>()</td><td>Parentheses define scope and precedence of elements
(gray)|(grey) matches gray or grey</td></tr>
</table>

Wildcards are used for file matching and they are absolute in that “*” matches any size string and “.” matches a single period. You can also match part of a string as in “file*.asm”. Quantification, OR, and Grouping operations do not apply when using wildcards with bash to specify specific files.

The single character “*” matches any size string. The string may contain periods. The components of regular expressions, including the wildcards, are very useful for crafting applications that must be able to handle any legal input value, like input forms or web pages.

We’ll see wildcards again in Chapter 16, where we’ll use bash to catalog and sort file and directory *metadata* on a disk drive.

The DDD Debugger

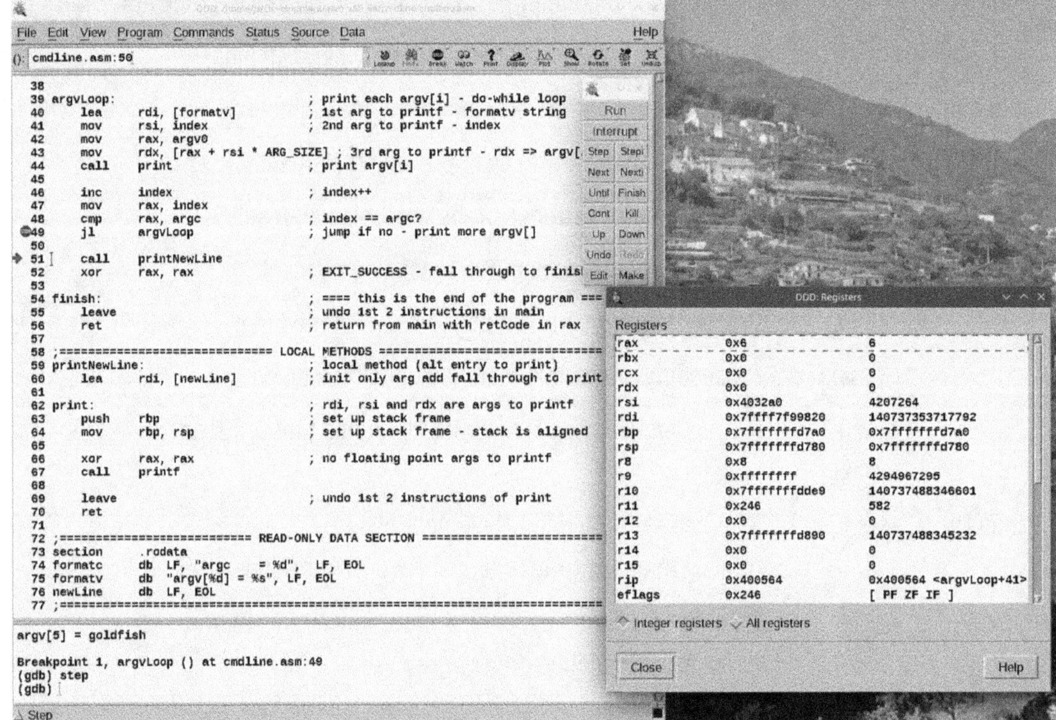

Figure 4-1. The loop has ended in cmdline.asm

Activities

1. Why did we xor rax with itself in line 30 of Listing 4-2?

2. Why did we xor rax with itself in line 52 of Listing 4-2?

3. Why did we xor eax with itself in line 66 of Listing 4-2?

4. Create a macro in macro.inc called zero. The macro should zero an arbitrary register as quickly as possible. Include macro.inc in cmdline.asm.

5. What is the difference between the registers eax and rax? Can you compare eax and rax? (i.e., cmp eax, rax)

6. List the registers (in order) that are used to pass arguments to a glibc subroutine.
7. If a single value is returned by a glibc function, where will your program find it?
8. Where are local variables (automatic variables) placed in memory?

CHAPTER 5

Using Macros and Passing Arguments on the Stack

So far, we've looked at assembly language programs that call the Linux kernel directly, and assembly language programs that call glibc. We're now going to look at assembly language methods that are callable from C or C++ programs. In Chapter 3, you wrote an assembly language program that has a main. In this chapter, we don't have the same program written in C and in assembly language. Instead, we have a C program that invokes the printEnv function. The printEnv method is in its own module environment.asm. It does not have a main. It also illustrates the nasm/yasm macro capability. Using the macro capability makes your assembly language programs start to look like a high-level language.

In Chapter 3, we discussed what to do if you have more than six arguments to a glibc method. We pass the first six arguments in the argument passing registers and then pass the rest of the arguments on the stack. The program environment.asm illustrates such a case.

Listing 5-1. environment.c

```
// environment.c
// John Schwartzman, Forte Systems, Inc.
// 05/08/2023

#include <time.h>                              // declaration of time
```


J. Schwartzman, *Assembly Language Reimagined*, https://doi.org/10.1007/979-8-8688-1724-3_5

```

int printenv(const char* dateTimeStr);     // declaration of asm function

int main(void)
{
    time_t  now;
    char*   dateTimeStr;

    time(&now);
    strTime = ctime(&now);
   return printenv(dateTimeStr);         // call printenv with dateTimeStr
}
```

Listing 5-2. environment.asm

```
;==========================================================================
; environment.asm - demonstrates invoking getenv, printf and strncpy
; environment.asm is called by environment.c (environment.c has main())
; environment.asm does not have a main. It exports the function with the
; declaration: int printenv(const char* dateTimeStr);
; John Schwartzman, Forte Systems, Inc.
; 05/08/2023
; linux x86_64
;
;========================= CONSTANT DEFINITIONS ==========================
BUFF_SIZE     equu    128          ; number of bytes in buffer
LF            equ      10          ; ASCII line feed character
EOL           equ       0          ; end of line character
TAB           equ       9          ; ASCII tab character
NUM_PUSH      equ       9          ; we PUSH 9 addresses for call
                                     to printf

;========================= MACRO DEFINITION ===========================
%macro getSaveEnv1                 ;=== getSaveEnv macro takes 1 arg ===
     lea      rdi, [env%1]         ; env%1 = ASCIIZ env var name
```

```
        call    getenv                  ; getenv will return with [rax]
                                          => ASCIIZ
        lea     rdi, [buf%1]            ; buf%1 = env var dest- 1st arg
                                          to strncpy
        mov     rsi, rax                ; [rsi] => ASCIIZ src - 2nd arg
                                          to strncpy
        mov     rdx, BUFF_SIZE - 1      ; rdx = max # to copy - 3rd arg
                                          to strncpy
        lea     rcx, [nullLine]         ; [rcx] => "(null)"
        or      rax, rax                ; did we get an invalid value
                                          (rax == 0)?
        cmovz   rsi, rcx                ; if yes, strncpy "(null)"
        call    strncpy                 ; call C library function to
                                          save env var
%endmacro                               ;===== end of getSaveEnv macro =====

;=========================== CODE SECTION ==============================
section         .text                    ;========== CODE SECTION ==========
global          printenv                 ; tell gcc linker we're
                                           exporting prntenv
extern          getenv, printf, strncpy ; tell assembler/linker about
                                            externals
                                         ; this module doesn't have _start
                                           or main

;========================= EXPORTED FUNCTION ========================
printenv:
        push    rbp                      ; set up stack frame
        mov     rbp, rsp                 ; set up stack frame - stack
                                           now aligned

        push   rdi                       ; save arg (dateStr)

        ; get and save environment variables by using macro for each env var
```

```
    getSaveEnv HOME
    getSaveEnv HOSTNAME
    getSaveEnv HOSTTYPE
    getSaveEnv CPU
    getSaveEnv PWD
    getSaveEnv TERM
    getSaveEnv PATH
    getSaveEnv SHELL
    getSaveEnv EDITOR
    getSaveEnv MAIL
    getSaveEnv LANG
    getSaveEnv PS1
    getSaveEnv HISTFILE

    ; call printf with many, many arguments
    ; pass args in RDI, RSI, RDX, RCX, R8 and R9 with remaining args on stack
    lea     rdi, [formatString]         ;  1st printf arg
    pop     rsi                         ;  2rd print arg (dateStr)
    lea     rdx, [bufHOME]              ;  3rd printf arg
    lea     rcx, [bufHOSTNAME]          ;  4th printf arg
    lea     r8,  [bufHOSTTYPE]          ;  5th printf arg
    lea     r9,  [bufCPU]               ;  6th printf arg
    ; we've used all 6 argument passing registers - PUSH remaining 9 args
    ; NOTE: PUSHes performed in reverse order because
    ;       args are read from top of stack! The stack grows downward!
    push    bufHISTFILE                 ; 15th printf arg
    push    bufPS1                      ; 14th printf arg
    push    bufLANG                     ; 13th printf arg
    push    bufMAIL                     ; 12th printf arg
    push    bufEDIT                     ; 11th printf arg
    push    bufSHELL                    ; 10th printf arg
    push    bufPATH                     ;  9th printf arg
```

```
        push     bufTERM                            ;  8th printf arg
        push     bufPWD                             ;  7th printf arg
        xor      eax, eax                           ; no floating point arguments
        call     printf                             ; invoke glibc to print
        xor      eax, eax                           ; return EXIT_SUCCESS = 0
        leave                      ; undo 1st 2 instructions - this will restore stack
        ret                        ; return to caller (main)
;===================== READ-ONLY DATA SECTION =======================
section        .rodata
formatString   db LF,  "Environment Variables on %s",
                       db TAB, "HOME     = %s",              LF
                       db TAB, "HOSTNAME = %s",              LF
                       db TAB, "HOSTTYPE = %s",              LF
                       db TAB, "CPU      = %s",              LF
                       db TAB, "PWD      = %s",              LF
                       db TAB, "TERM     = %s",              LF
                       db TAB, "PATH     = %s",              LF
                       db TAB, "SHELL    = %s",              LF
                       db TAB, "EDITOR   = %s",              LF
                       db TAB, "MAIL     = %s",              LF,
                       db TAB, "LANG     = %s",              LF,
                       db TAB, "PS1      = %s",              LF,
                       db TAB, "HISTFILE = %s",          LF, LF, EOL
envHOME                db "HOME",                            EOL
envHOSTNAME            db "HOSTNAME",                        EOL
envHOSTTYPE            db "HOSTTYPE",                        EOL
envCPU                 db "CPU",                             EOL
envPWD                 db "PWD",                             EOL
```

```
envTERM               db "TERM",                              EOL
envPATH               db "PATH",                              EOL
envSHELL              db "SHELL",                             EOL
envEDITOR             db "EDITOR",                            EOL
envMAIL               db "MAIL",                              EOL
envLANG               db "LANG",                              EOL
envPS1                db "PS1",                               EOL
envHISTFILE           db "HISTFILE",                          EOL

nullLine              db "(null)",                            EOL
newLine               db                                      LF, EOL
;====================== UNINITIALIZED DATA SECTION ==================
section               .bss
bufHOME               resb                  BUFF_SIZE
bufHOSTNAME           resb                  BUFF_SIZE
bufHOSTTYPE           resb                  BUFF_SIZE
bufCPU                resb                  BUFF_SIZE
bufPWD                resb                  BUFF_SIZE
bufTERM               resb                  BUFF_SIZE
bufPATH               resb                  BUFF_SIZE
bufSHELL              resb                  BUFF_SIZE
bufEDITOR             resb                  BUFF_SIZE
bufMAIL               resb                  BUFF_SIZE
bufLANG               resb                  BUFF_SIZE
bufPS1                resb                  BUFF_SIZE
bufHISTFILE           resb                  BUFF_SIZE
;====================================================================
```

If you look at environment.c (Listing 5-1), you'll see that we have put in a declaration for printEnv (line 7). The declaration is to keep the c compiler from complaining when it encounters the printEnv instruction in line 16. If we had a lot of methods to export, we'd put them in a C header file.

The main function of environment.c gets the current time as a string and calls printEnv(timeString). It then returns to Linux the return value it obtained from printEnv.

The file environment.asm is designed to show you how to pass more than six arguments to a function. If you look at Listing 5-2, you'll note that the format string (line 89) that we pass as the first parameter to printenv has fourteen string placeholders. That means that we're going to pass a total of fifteen arguments to printf. We know that we can only pass six arguments in registers, so the remaining nine arguments are passed on the stack.

The first thing that we do inside printenv is to push its only parameter onto the stack (line 41) because we need rdi for other things. Then we need to do the same thing (call getenv and call strncpy) thirteen times. For that we are going to use the macro capability of yasm. The macro getSaveEnv is defined outside of our program in lines 18–28). It takes an environment name string as its only argument. The first time we call our macro (line 44), we pass the argument HOME which the macro interprets as envHOME. The program defines the environment name strings as a collection of bytes in lines 104–116. The first thing the macro does is to load rdi with the environment name string (line 19). It then calls the glibc function char* getenv(char* name) in line 20. The function getenv() will return the addresss of a buffer containing the environment variable. It will return NULL (0) if it can't find that environment name. The macro then marshals the arguments for the glibc function char* strncpy(char* dest, char* src, size_t maxNumCharToCopy). Because maxNumCharToCopy is one less than the size of the destination buffer, we're protected from the case where the size of dest is greater than the size of its storage location. If we'd used char* strcpy(char* dest, char* src), we wouldn't have that protection and our program could blow up.

The next action of the macro is to handle the case where getenv returns NULL. If getenv returns NULL, we want to print the string "(null)". We load rcx with the address of nullLine (line 24) and then test whether rax (the address returned by getenv) contains zero. We OR rax with itself (line 25) and then we use the cmovz rsi, rcx instruction. The or instruction leaves rax alone but will set the rflags value ZF = 1 if rax was zero. The cmovz instruction will only move rcx into rsi if ZF = 1, but rsi already contains the value returned by getenv in rax. The result is that if rsi contains zero, cmovz rsi, rcx moves [nullLine] to rsi, otherwise cmovz does nothing.

We invoke our macro thirteen times in lines 44–56 and then we marshal our fifteen arguments for the single call to printf. The data pointed to by formatString is the first argument to printf. Remember that before we used our macro thirteen times, we had pushed the buffer pointing to our dateTimeString onto the stack. Well, its time to recover it. In line 61, we execute the instruction pop rsi.

Even though we pushed rdi to the stack, we pop rsi from the stack, because it now becomes the second argument to printf. Here we use the stack to copy the contents of rdi into rsi.

We now marshal the next four arguments into the argument passing registers, and we're ready to push the remaining strings onto the stack. Note that we push them in reverse order. The stack is last-in-first-out (LIFO) structure. The last value pushed will be the first value popped.

Finally, we set the 32-bit register eax to zero (xor eax, eax in line 79). The glibc printf method uses rax to tell it whether there are floating point arguments in our format string. If rax is set to zero, there are no floating point arguments. Then we call printf and we're done.

If you are missing some of the fourteen environment variables, go into your ~/.bashrc file and add a few. Add a statement like export EDITOR='/usr/bin/nano'. Just remember to close any open terminal windows before trying again. Bash must restart in order to load all of its configuration files.

More About Macros

We can make our assembly language a little bit more like a high-level language by adding other macros to our .asm modules. We usually put all of our macros in a macro.inc include file. Take a look at the following example.

In order to ask glibc to perform a strlen instruction, we do something like this every time we need a strlen:

```
extern strlen
...
lea       rdi, [exampleString]
call      strlen
...
```

We can make our code look more like a high-level language by doing something like this:

```
strlen    [exampleString]
```

In order to get there, we create a macro file that looks like this:

```
; from macro.inc
...
extern  strlen
...
%macro strlen 0
       call     strlen
%endmacro

%macro strlen 1
       lea      rdi, %1
       strlen
%endmacro
```

Here we have the macro strlen which takes no arguments and calls the glibc function, strlen. That's not very useful because we always need to load the string we're interested in into the first argument passing register, rdi.

This will now work, but it takes two instructions:

```
        lea     rdi, [exampleString]
        strlen
```

We get around this difficulty by overloading the strlen macro. The original macro takes no arguments. We'll overload this macro with a version that takes one argument and calls the original zero-argument macro:

```
%macro strlen 1
        lea     rdi, %1
        strlen
%endmacro
```

Now, whenever we need to call strlen, we include macro.inc and simply write

```
        strlen [exampleString]
```

The one-argument macro sets rdi to the correct argument, %1, and then calls the no argument version of the macro. This makes it look as if we're programming in a high-level language.

Syntax problems in macro.inc can cause strange and misleading error messages. When I've mistyped a function name, I've often found that the labels in my calling program stop being recognized. If you see error messages like this, look closely at your include file, macro.inc.

Activities

1. We learned that it is the responsibility of the calling function to remove parameters passed on the stack. Does printenv() satisfy this requirement? How and where is it satisfied?
2. The program environment.asm is long and complicated because it was written to demonstrate passing parameters on the stack. Simplify it by calling printf() immediately for every environment variable you get. Use the macro language capability in your solution. Hint: Rewrite the macro getSaveEnv to change strncpy into printf. Name your program env.asm.
3. Why do we prefer instructions like xor rax, rax to instructions like mov rax, 0? The latter seems more self-explanatory than the former.
4. Why do we prefer instructions like or rax, rax to instructions like cmp rax, 0? The latter seems more self-explanatory than the former.
5. Macros are hard to follow in the debugger. Try opening View ➤ Machine Code Window when you debug. Use the Stepi button to Step into the machine code.
6. Macros are hard to follow in the source code. Listing files can be created that expand the macros into the macros in the body of the code. Makefile produces listing files like environment.lst. Print environment.lst to see if it helps you follow the macro code.

7. The program random.c requires the user to repeatedly guess a random number. Create random.asm and implement a main function that will initialize randomization and invoke guessNumber(). Remember to comment out the main in random.c.

8. Useful utility department: Rename your env program to <your initials>env and copy it to /usr/local/bin. Make sure that the new executable is on the path.

9. Why do we copy <your initials>env to /usr/local/bin?

10. Add an install target to Makefile so that it copies <your initials>env to /usr/local/bin.

11. If necessary, modify ~/.bashrc so that all of the variables referenced by <your initials>env are not null.

12. Add the glibc functions strcpy and strncpy to macro.inc. Prepare a small assembly language program to demonstrate these functions. How did you decide which registers to use?

13. Why is strncpy a "safer" instruction than strcpy?

CHAPTER 6

Conditional Compilation and Conditional Build

We'll now consider how to assemble, compile, and build a specific version of a program. The file minmax.c (Listing 6-1) contains code that makes it compile differently based on whether or not the variable C_VERSION is defined at build time. If C_VERSION is defined, lines 12–25 are compiled, otherwise lines 28–29 are compiled. The main() function gets its definition of printMin and printMax based on which section is active. If C_VERSION is defined, min and max are defined as macros, and printMin and printMax are implemented using min and max within the c program. If C_VERSION is not defined, we have only declarations of printMin and printMax. The actual implementation is provided by the linker using minmax.obj at build time.

How do we choose which way we want to compile? Makefile (Listing 6-3) contains ifeq ($(DEF), C_VERSION). We can see that there are two ways to compile this project. If you issue the command "make DEF=C_VERSION", you don't assemble minmax.asm, but you do compile minmax.c using "gcc -D $(DEF) $(PROG).c". The -D option is used to define C_VERSION for the compilation of minmax.c.

The way in which you invoke Makefile determines how your program will be built.

Listing 6-1. minmax.c

```
1 // minmax.c
2 // John Schwartzman, Forte Systems, Inc.
3 // 05/15/2023
4 // x86_64
5
6 #include <stdlib.h>     // dec of atol; def of EXIT_SUCCESS, EXIT_FAILURE
7 #include <stdio.h>      // declaration of printf
8
```


J. Schwartzman, *Assembly Language Reimagined*, https://doi.org/10.1007/979-8-8688-1724-3_6

```
#ifdef C_VERSION        // implement these macros and functions in c

  #define max(a, b) ((a) > (b) ? (a) : (b))   // C macro
  #define min(a, b) ((a) < (b) ? (a) : (b))   // C macro

  long printMax(long a, long b)       // implement c function printMax
  {
      printf("\nmax(%ld, %ld) = %ld\n", a, b, max(a, b));
  }

 long printMin(long a, long b)       // implement c function printMin
 {
    printf("\nmin(%ld, %ld) = %ld\n\n", a, b, min(a, b));
 }

#else   // c_version is not defined we declare these external functions

  long printMax(long a, long b);      // declare external function printMax
  long printMin(long a, long b);      // declare external function printMin

#endif                                // end of conditional compilation

int main(int argc, char* argv[])
{
  if (argc == 3)  // get arguments from command line and make them longs
  {
      long a = atol(argv[1]);    // values on the command line are char*
      long b = atol(argv[2]);   // values on the command line are char*
      printMax(a, b);
      printMin(a, b);
      return EXIT_SUCCESS;
  }
  else
```

```
    {
        printf("USAGE: Please enter 2 long integers on the command line"
               " following the program name.\n\n");
        return EXIT_FAILURE;
    }
}
```

Listing 6-2. minmax.asm

```
;==========================================================================
; minmax.asm - demonstrates using macros for code and for local variables
; John Schwartzman, Forte Systems, Inc.
; 05/14/2023
; linux x86_64
;
;======================== CONSTANT DEFINITIONS ======================
LF              equu    10          ; ASCII linefeed character
EOL             equ      0          ; end of line character
VAR_SIZE        equ      8          ; each local var is 8 bytes
NUM_VAR         equ      2          ; number local var (round up to even num)

;====================== DEFINE LOCAL VARIABLES ======================
%define         a           qword [rsp + VAR_SIZE * (NUM_VAR - 2)]    ; rsp + 0
%define         b           qword [rsp + VAR_SIZE * (NUM_VAR - 1)]    ; rsp + 8

;========================== DEFINE MACRO ============================
%macro prologue  0                  ;=== prologue macro takes 0 arguments ===
     push       rbp                 ; set up stack frame
     mov        rbp, rsp            ; set up stack frame - stack now aligned
     sub        rsp, VAR_SIZE * NUM_VAR   ; make space for local variables on stack
```

```
        mov     a, rdi              ; rdi contains a - 1st arg to min or max
        mov     b, rsi              ; rsi contains b - 2nd arg to min or max
        mov     rsi, a              ; 2nd arg to printf = a
        mov     rdx, b              ; 3rd arg to printf = b
        mov     rcx, ri             ; 4th arg to printf = a; assume result=a
        cmp     rcx, b              ; compare a to b - only changes flags reg
%endmacro                           ;====== end of prologue macro =====

;========================== DEFINE MACRO ==============================
%macro epilogue  0                  ;=== epilogue macro takes 0 arguments ===
        xor     rax, rax            ; tell printf no floating point args
        push    rcx                 ; save rcx in order to return it
        call    printf              ; invoke the C function
        pop     rax                 ; rax = return ; we PUSH rcx, but POP rax
        leave                       ; undo 1st 2 prologue instructions
        ret                         ; return to caller
%endmacro                           ;====== end of epilogue macro =====

;========================== DEFINE MACRO ==============================
%macro max      0                   ;====== max macro takes 0 args ====
        cmovb   rcx, b              ; return value = rcx = b (if a < b)
        lea     rdi, [formatStrMax] ; 1st arg to printf
%endmacro                           ;========= end of max macro =======

;========================== DEFINE MACRO ==============================
%macro min      0                   ;====== min macro takes 0 args ====
        cmova   rcx, b              ; return value = rcx = b if (a > b)
        lea     rdi, [formatStrMin] ; 1st arg to printf
```

```
%endmacro                                  ;======= end of min macro =========

;=========================== CODE SECTION ==============================
section         .text
global          printMax, printMin ; tell linker about exported functions
extern          printf             ; tell assembler/linker about externals

printMax:                                  ;======= printMax function =======
     prologue
     max
     epilogue                              ;==== end of printMax function ====

printMin:                                  ;======= printMin function =======
     prologue
     min
     epilogue                              ;==== end of printMin function ====

;==================== READ-ONLY DATA SECTION =======================
section         .rodata
formatStrMax    db            "max(%ld, %ld) = %ld", LF, EOL
formatStrMin    db            "min(%ld, %ld) = %ld", LF, LF, EOL
;======================================================================
```

Listing 6-3. Makefile for minmax

```
#######################################################################
#
#     Makefile for minmax
#     John Schwartzman, Forte Systems, Inc.
#     05/15/2023
#
#     Commands:  make DEF=C_VERSION will build a.out only
#                make .debug will build minmax (minmax.c and minmax.asm)
#     Requires:  ../maketest.sh
#
```

```
#########################################################################
PROG  := minmax
SHELL := /bin/bash

ifeq ($(DEF), C_VERSION)      ##### BUILD a.out #####

.release: $(PROG).c Makefile
	$(info "Building a.out only...")
	@source ../maketest.sh && test .release .debug
	gcc -D $(DEF) $(PROG).c

.debug: $(PROG).c $(PROG).c Makefile
	$(info "Building a.out only...")
	@source ../maketest.sh && test .debug .release
	gcc -D $(DEF) $(PROG).c

else     ##### BUILD minmax #####

.release: $(PROG).c $(PROG).asm Makefile
	@source ../maketest.sh && test .release .debug
	$(info "Building minmax...")
	yasm -f elf64 -o $(PROG).obj -l $(PROG).lst $(PROG).asm
	gcc -z noexecstack -no-pie $(PROG).c $(PROG).obj -o $(PROG)

.debug: $(PROG).c $(PROG).c Makefile
	$(info "Building minmax...")
	@source ../maketest.sh && test .debug .release
	yasm -f elf64 -g dwarf2 -o $(PROG).obj -l $(PROG).lst $(PROG).asm
	gcc -g -z noexecstack -no-pie $(PROG).c $(PROG).obj -o $(PROG)

endif     ##### end of conditional build #####

clean:
	rm -f $(PROG) $(PROG).obj $(PROG).lst a.out .debug .release
#########################################################################
```

In the file minmax.asm (Listing 6-2), we play around with assembler macros to try to minimize the differences between printMax and printMin. It comes out like this:

prologue:

standard method prologue

leave space for local variables a and b

place args in local variables

marshal a and b for printf (2nd and 3rd args)

rcx = a

compare a to b

max:	min:
cmovb rcx, b; if a < b then rcx = b	cmova rcx, b; if a > b then rcx = b
marshal 1st arg for printf (formatStrMax)	marshal 1st arg for printf (formatStrMin)

epilogue:

rax = 0

push rcx ;save result rcx on stack

call printf

pop rax ;restore result from stack

standard method epilogue

In other words:

1. We set everything up.
2. We move the answer to rcx.
3. We push rcx to the stack.
4. We call printf.
5. We restore the pushed value into rax.
6. We return the answer.
7. We tear everything down.

The DDD Debugger

Figure 6-1 shows DDD waiting at a breakpoint at max in printMax. We invoked ddd using the command

```
ddd --args minmax 39 41
```

Whenever we want to pass information to a program running under DDD, we use the command

```
ddd -args <program-name> <arg1> <arg2> … <argn>
```

Note from the Machine Code window that we are about to execute cmovb rcx, b. The stack shows that a equals 39 and b equals 41. Is b going to be moved to rcx? Since a < b, the answer is yes.

Notice how we display the contents of the stack: select Data ➤ Memory from the DDD menu and "Examine 2 decimal giants from $rsp". A giant is an 8-byte (64-bit) qword. We want to show two base-10 giants from the memory pointed to by the stack pointer register (rsp). Click the Print or Display button to show the contents of memory.

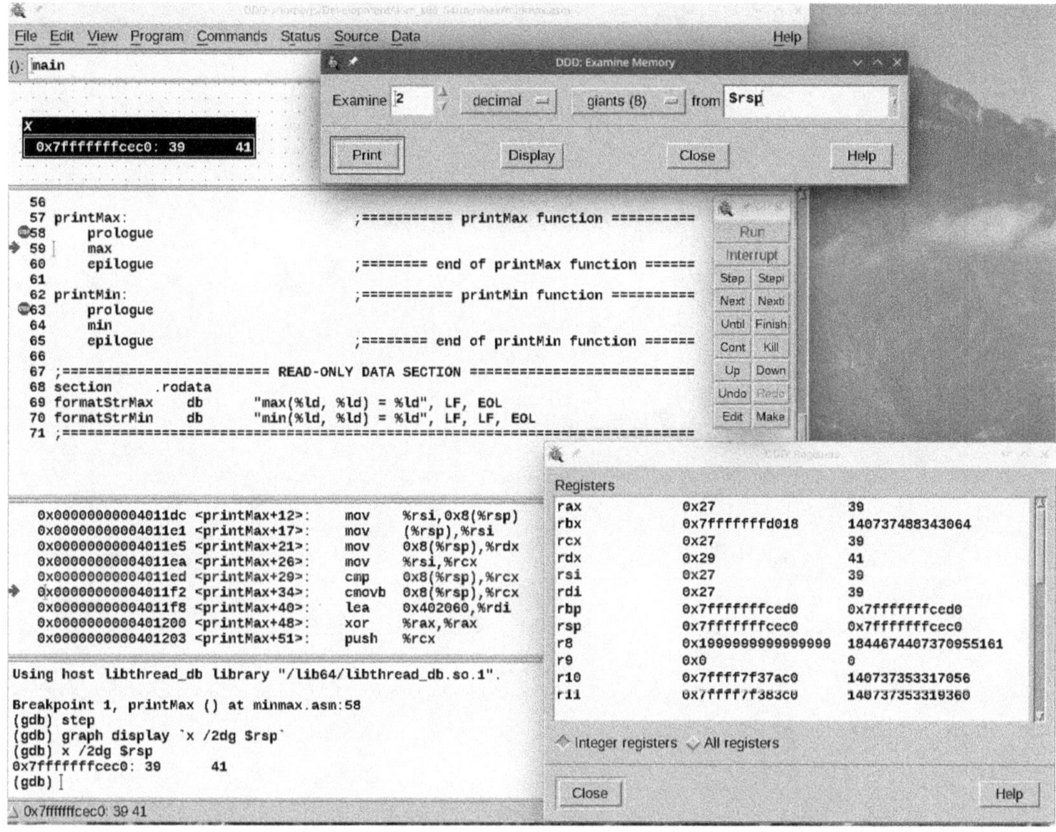

***Figure 6-1.** DDD is about to execute cmovb rcx, b*

Activities

1. Run minmax in DDD and verify that minmax.c allows you to view local variables directly, by hovering the cursor over a and b in the program listing.
2. View the parameters argc and argv in minmax.c using DDD.
3. Rewrite minmax.asm without using assembly language macros.

CHAPTER 7

Recursion

The mathematical sequence factorial is defined recursively as

```
f(n) =  {
        1 if n <= 1,
        n * f(n - 1) if n > 1
        }
```

We're now going to create the recursive function factorial both in c and in assembly language. The trick to programming recursively is to keep calling the recursive case until you reach the base case where f(n) = 1. The file factorial.c is shown in Listing 7-1, and factorial.asm is shown in Listing 7-2.

The way in which you invoke Makefile (Listing 7-3) determines how minmax.asm will be built.

Listing 7-1. factorial.c

```
// factorial.c
// John Schwartzman, Forte Systems, Inc.
// 05/17/2023

#define MAX_INT 20

#include<stdio.h> // for printf and scanf

#if defined(__COMMA__)

        int commaSeparate(long n, char* buffer); // declaration of asm function

#endif //__COMMA__

// recursive function to compute factorial of n
long factorial(int n)
```


J. Schwartzman, *Assembly Language Reimagined*, https://doi.org/10.1007/979-8-8688-1724-3_7

```
{
        if (n == 1) // base case
        {
                return 1;
        }
        else
        {
                return (n * factorial(n - 1));
        }
}

int main()
{
int nRetVal = 0;
int n;
long fact;

do
{
        printf("\nEnter a positive integer less than or equal to %d: ",
        MAX_INT);
        scanf("%d", &n);
}
while (n < 1 || n > MAX_INT);

fact = factorial(n);
printf("%d! = %ld\n", n, fact);

#if defined(__COMMA__)

        char buffer[32];
        nRetVal = commaSeparate(fact, buffer);
        printf("%d! = %s\n\n", n, buffer);

#endif //__COMMA__

        return nRetVal;
}
```

Listing 7-2. factorial.asm

```
;==========================================================================
; factorial.asm
; John Schwartzman, Forte Systems, Inc.
; 05/28/2023
; Linux x86_64
;
;========================= CONSTANT DEFINITIONS =======================
LF              equ     10                      ; ASCII linefeed character
EOL             equ      0                      ; end of line character
ONE             equ      1                      ; number 1
VAR_SIZE        equ      8                      ; each local var is 8 bytes
NUM_VAR         equ      2                      ; number local var (round up to even num)
MAX_INPUT       equ     20                      ; max size input
EXIT_FAILURE    equ      1                      ; return 1 to indicate failure

;============================ DEFINE MACRO ============================
%macro      zero    1
      xor     %1, %1
%endmacro

;======================= DEFINE LOCAL VARIABLES =======================
%define     n      qword [rsp + VAR_SIZE * (NUM_VAR - 2)]     ; rsp + 0
%define     fact   qword [rsp + VAR_SIZE * (NUM_VAR - 1)]     ; rsp + 8

;=========================== CODE SECTION =============================
section     .text                   ;========== CODE SECTION ==========
global      main                    ; tell linker about export
extern      scanf, printf           ; tell assembler/linker about externals

```

```
%ifdef __COMMA__                        ;======= use commaSeparate ========
    extern      commaSeparate
%endif                                  ;==================================

main:
    push    rbp
    mov     rbp, rsp
    sub     rsp, NUM_VAR * VAR_SIZE ; make space on stack for n and fact var.

    lea     rdi, [promptFmt]        ; 1st arg to printf
    zero    rax
    call    printf                  ; prompt user

    lea     rdi, [scanfFmt]         ; 1st arg to scanf
    lea     rsi, n                  ; 2nd arg to scanf - where to place input
    zero    rax                     ; no floating point args to scanf
    call    scanf                   ; get x

    cmp     n, MAX_INPUT            ; legal input?
    jg      badInput                ;    jump if no
    jmp     continue                ; skip over badInput section

badInput:
    lea     rdi, [wrongInputStr]    ; report bad input and exit
    zero    rax
    call    printf
    mov     rax, EXIT_FAILURE
    jmp     fin

continue:
    mov     rdi, n                  ; save x
    call    factorial
    mov     fact, rax               ; save factorial of x
```

```

        lea     rdi, [outputFmt]        ; 1st arg to printf
        mov     rsi, n                  ; 2nd arg to printf
        mov     rdx, fact               ; 3rd arg to printf
        zero    rax                     ; no floating point args to printf
        call    printf                  ; print result

%ifdef __COMMA__                        ; == DISPLAY RESULT with commaSeparate ==

        mov     rdi, fact               ; 1st and only arg to commaSeparate
        lea     rsi, [buffer]
        call    commaSeparate

        lea     rdi, [outputFmtCommma]  ; 1st arg to printf
        mov     rsi, n                  ; 2nd arg to printf
        lea     rdx, [buffer]           ; 3rd arg to printf
        zero    rax                     ; no floating point args to printf
        call    printf                  ; print "x! = " followed by result

%endif                                  ; == DISPLAY RESULT with comma Separate ==

        zero    rax                     ; return EXIT_SUCCESS

fin:
        leave
        ret

;====================== DEFINE LOCAL VARIABLE ======================
;%define    n    qword [rsp + VAR_SIZE * (NUM_VAR - 2)]        ; rsp + 0

;========================== CODE SECTION ===========================
factorial:
```

```
        push    rbp
        mov     rbp, rsp
        sub     rsp, NUM_VAR * VAR_SIZE ; make space for n

        cmp     rdi, ONE                ; base case?
        jg      greater                 ;    jump if no
        mov     rax, ONE                ; the answer to the base case

        leave
        ret

greater:
        mov     n, rdi                  ; save n
        dec     rdi                     ; call factorial with n - 1
        call    factorial               ; recursive call to factorial

        mov     rdi, n                  ; restore original n
        imul    rax, rdi                ; multiply factorial(n - 1) * n

        leave
        ret

;===========================  DATA SECTION ============================
section       .data
buffer        times 32 db 0                         ; char buffer[32]

;===================== READ-ONLY DATA SECTION ========================
section          .rodata
scanfFmt         db          "%ld", EOL
promptFmt        db          LF, "Enter a positive integer from 1 to 20: ", EOL
outputFmt        db          "%ld! = %ld", LF, EOL
outputFmtCommma db           "%ld! = %s", LF, EOL
```

```
wrongInputStr   db          "You have entered an invalid number.", LF, LF, EOL

;=====================================================================
```

Listing 7-3. Makefile for factorial

```
########################################################################
#
#    Makefile for factorial
#    05/28/2023
#
#    Commands:    make [DEF=__COMMA__] [.release]
#                 make [DEF=__COMMA__] .debug
#                 make clean
#  Requires:  ../maketest.sh
#
########################################################################
PROG  := factorial
SHELL := /bin/bash
EXT   := ../commaSeparate/commaSeparate

ifeq ($(DEF), __COMMA__)     ######### use commaSeparate for output ##########

.release: $(PROG).asm $(EXT).asm $(PROG).c Makefile
   $(info ##### release __COMMA__ build #####)
   @source ../maketest.sh && test .release .debug
   yasm -f elf64 $(EXT).asm -o commaSeparate.obj
   yasm -D $(DEF) -f elf64 $(PROG).asm -o $(PROG).obj
   gcc -z noexecstack $(PROG).obj commaSeparate.obj -o $(PROG)
   gcc -Wall -O3 -z noexecstack -D $(DEF) $(PROG).c commaSeparate.obj

debug: $(PROG).asm Makefile $(EXT).asm $(PROG).c Makefile
   $(info ##### debug __COMMA__ build #####)
   @source ../maketest.sh && test .debug .release
```

```
	yasm -f elf64 -g dwarf2 -o commaSeparate.obj $(EXT).asm
	yasm -D $(DEF) -f elf64 -g dwarf2 -o $(PROG).obj $(PROG).asm
	gcc -g -z noexecstack $(PROG).obj commaSeparate.obj -o $(PROG)
	gcc -g -z noexecstack -D $(DEF) $(PROG).c commaSeparate.obj

else 		############### output normally #################

.release: $(PROG).asm Makefile $(PROG).c
	@source ../maketest.sh && test .release .debug
	yasm -f elf64 -o $(PROG).obj -l $(PROG).lst $(PROG).asm
	gcc -z noexecstack $(PROG).obj -o $(PROG)
	gcc -Wall -O3 $(PROG).c

.debug: $(PROG).asm Makefile $(PROG).c
	@source ../maketest.sh && test .debug .release
	yasm -f elf64 -g dwarf2 -o $(PROG).obj -l $(PROG).lst $(PROG).asm
	gcc -g -z noexecstack $(PROG).obj -o $(PROG)
	gcc -g $(PROG).c

endif 	##################### use commaSeparate #######################

clean:
	@rm -f $(PROG) *.obj a.out *.lst .debug .release
######################################################################
```

Both source files and Makefile use the variable __COMMA__ for conditional compilation, but we won't use this feature until Chapter 9.

When we call the recursive function, we don't exit from the function. Instead, we establish another stack frame and call the recursive function from within the recursive function. The stack keeps growing until we reach our base case and get a definite answer to the f(1) case (f(1) = 1). At this point the stack unwinds, call by call, multiplication by multiplication, until we are left with a final answer to the factorial of f(n).

Run both programs and ensure that they provide the same result:

```
js@suse-tumbleweed-z4:~/Development/asm_x86_64/factorial$ ./factorial

Enter a positive integer from 1 to 20: 20
20! = 2432902008176640000
js@suse-tumbleweed-z4:~/Development/asm_x86_64/factorial$ ./a.out

Enter a positive integer from 1 to 20: 20
20! = 2432902008176640000
```

Well we've got an answer, but it's not very easy to read. We'll fix this with the commaSeparate utility program in Chapter 9.

Activities

1. Why are we restricted to a maximum input of 20 when obtaining the value of a factorial? Suggest a way to raise the maximum input. Implement your solution.
2. Write the declaration of scanf. Why is scanf a *varadic* function?
3. Write a small assembly language example of a call to scanf. Assume that you are calling scanf to populate an automatic (stack-based) variable. Show the marshaling of your variable.
4. Write a program in C, C++, or assembly language that finds the nth term of a Fibonacci sequence. Your program should implement a recursive (divide and conquer) solution.
5. Describe what is placed on the stack before each recursive call to factorial. How does factorial use the value(s) on the stack?

CHAPTER 8

Using Floating Point Registers

We're now going to resurrect the cmdline program from Chapter 4. In that program, we passed some string parameters into the program on the command line. This time we're going to pass in some string parameters, but we'll treat them as doubles and get their values using the glibc function atof() (atof stands for ASCII to float). We'll read in some values and treat them as doubles (32-bit values). To do that, we need to use one of the floating point registers, xmm0.

Listing 8-1. sum.c

```
// sum.c - retrieve floats from cmdline
// John Schwartzman, Forte Systems, Inc.
// 06/05/2023

#include <stdio.h>        // declares printf
#include <stdlib.h>       // defines EXIT_SUCCESS - declaration of atof

int main(int argc, char* argv[])
{
        double sum = 0.0;
        double val;

       printf("\nargc    =  %d\n", argc);                        // print argc
       for (int i = 1; i < argc; i++)
       {
           val = atof(argv[i]);
```


J. Schwartzman, *Assembly Language Reimagined*, https://doi.org/10.1007/979-8-8688-1724-3_8

```
        printf("argv[%d] = %s = %.2f\n", i, argv[i], val); // print argv[i]
        sum += val;

    }
    printf("\nsum = %.2f\n\n", sum);                        // print sum
    return EXIT_SUCCESS;
}
```

Here is the program in assembly language.

Listing 8-2. sum.asm

```
;=====================================================================
; sum.asm - retrieve floats from cmdline and compute sum of floats
; John Schwartzman, Forte Systems, Inc.
; 06/07/2023
; linux x86_64
;
;======================== CONSTANT DEFINITIONS =======================
LF              equu     10          ; ASCII linefeed char
EOL             equ       0          ; end of line
ARG_SIZE        equ       8          ; size of argv vector & size of a push
VAR_SIZE        equ       8          ; each local var is 8 bytes
NUM_VAR         equ       6          ; number local var (round up to even num)

;====================== DEFINE LOCAL VARIABLES =======================
%define      index       qword [rsp + VAR_SIZE * (NUM_VAR - 6)] ; rsp +  0
%define      argc        qword [rsp + VAR_SIZE * (NUM_VAR - 5)] ; rsp +  8
%define      argv0       qword [rsp + VAR_SIZE * (NUM_VAR - 4)] ; rsp + 16
%define      sum         qword [rsp + VAR_SIZE * (NUM_VAR - 3)] ; rsp + 24
```

```
%define      tmpR12      qword [rsp + VAR_SIZE * (NUM_VAR - 2)] ; rsp + 32

;========================== CODE SECTION =============================
section      .text
global       main                    ; gcc linker expects main, not _start
extern       printf, atof            ; tell linker about externals

main:                                ; program starts here
        push    rbp                  ; set up stack frame
        mov     rbp, rsp             ; set up stack frame - stack is aligned
        sub     rsp, NUM_VAR * VAR_SIZE  ; make space for local variables
                                     ; set local variables
        pxor    xmm0, xmm0           ; initialize xmm0 to 0.0
        movsd   sum, xmm0            ; save it in sum
        mov     index, 1             ; index = 1
        mov     argc, rdi            ; argc  = rdi (1st arg to main)
        mov     argv0, rsi           ; argv0 = rsi (2nd arg to main)
        mov     tmpR12, r12          ; r12 is callee saved reg we need

        lea     rdi, [newLine]       ; print blank line
        xor     rax, rax
        call    printf

argvLoop:                            ; print each argv[i] - do-while loop
        mov     rsi, index           ; 2nd arg to printf - index
        mov     rax, argv0
        mov     rdi, [rax + rsi * ARG_SIZE]  ; 3rd arg to printf - rdx => argv[i]
        mov     r12, rdi             ; save rdi to r12
        or      rdi, rdi             ; is there an argv[i]?
        jz      next                 ; jump if no
```

```
        call    atof                    ; double is placed in xmm0

next:
        movsd   xmm1, sum               ; xmm1 = sum
        addsd   xmm1, xmm0              ; xmm1 = xmm1 + xmm0
        movsd   sum, xmm1               ; save sum = xmm1

        lea     rdi, [formatVal]        ; 1st arg to printf - formatVal string
        mov     rsi, index              ; 2nd arg to printf - index
        mov     rdx, r12                ; 3rd arg to printf - restore rdx from r12
        call    printsd                 ; print argv[i]

        inc     index                   ; index++
        mov     rax, index
        cmp     rax, argc               ; index == argc?
        jl      argvLoop                ; jump if no - print more argv[]

        lea     rdi, [formatSum]        ; print sum
        movsd   xmm0, sum               ; sum must be in xmm0 for printf
        call    printsd

        xor     rax, rax                ; return EXIT_SUCCESS

finish:                                 ; === end of the program ===
        mov     r12, tmpR12             ; restore calee saved reg r12
        leave                           ; undo 1st 2 instructions in main
        ret                             ; return from main with retCode in rax

;========================== LOCAL METHODS ============================
printsd:                ; print sclar double - rdi, rsi and rdx are args to print
        push    rbp                     ; set up stack frame
```

```
80      mov     rbp, rsp                ; set up stack frame - stack is aligned
81
82      mov     rax, 1                  ; one floating point arg (Xmm0) to printf
83      call    printf
84
85      leave                           ; undo 1st 2 instructions of printsd
86      ret
87
88 ;======================= READ-ONLY DATA SECTION =====================
89 section        .rodata
90 formatVal      db      "argv[%d] = %s = %.2f", LF, EOL   ; double in xmm0
91 formatSum      db      LF, "sum     = %.2f", LF, LF, EOL ; double in xmm0
92 newLine        db      LF, EOL
93 ;====================================================================
```

The file sum.c is shown in Listing 8-1 and the file sum.asm is shown in Listing 8-2.

As usual, sum.c abstracts away the implementation details of the algorithm. It is only by looking at the machine code window in DDD while debugging a.out that we see that a different register is being employed than those we've used so far. We see values being transferred to and from register xmm0.

The xmm registers are the lower 128-bits of the 256-bit ymm registers, which are the lower 256-bits of the 512-bit zmm registers in the newer Intel x86_64 processors. These registers are used for single instructions mutiple data (SIMD) operations, which are useful for image processing, 3D rendering, video and sound applications, etc. We'll use the xmm registers, which are 128-bit floating point registers that can hold four float values or two double values.

The file sum.asm shows all the details of the implementation. We begin by checking the number of arguments on the command line. Remember that the 0th argument is the complete path of the program being executed. Then we loop through the string arguments and convert each one to a double by calling atof (line 49) whose prototype is double atof(const char* buffer). Calling atof reads through the buffer finding sign and decimal point values and places the resultant double in xmm0. We move sum to xmm1, add it to float(argv[i]) which is in xmm0, and place the result in sum.

Everything works as before. Integer arguments are passed in rdi, rsi, rdx, ..., but floating point variables must be placed in xmm0, xmm1, xmm2, ...

```
js@suse-tumbleweed-z4:~/Development/asm_x86_64/sum$ ./sum 123.4 456.7 789.5

argc    = 4
argv[1] = 123.4 = 123.40
argv[2] = 456.7 = 456.70
argv[3] = 789.5 = 789.50

sum     = 1369.60

js@suse-tumbleweed-z4:~/Development/asm_x86_64/sum$ ./a.out 123.4
456.7 789.5

argc    = 4
argv[1] = 123.4 = 123.40
argv[2] = 456.7 = 456.70
argv[3] = 789.5 = 789.50

sum     = 1369.60
```

Activities

1. Create the file createDataFile.asm. It should take a small set of numbers as strings from the command line and write each entry to the file calc.txt. Refer to cmdline.asm in Chapter 4 for guidance about processing each entry. Do something like this to write each entry to the output file calc.txt:

```
...
mov rcx, index
mov rax, argv0
mov rdi, fp ; 1st arg to fprintf - file pointer
lea rsi, [fmtPrint] ; 2nd arg to fprintf
```

```
mov rdx, [rax + rcx * ARG_SIZE] ; 3rd arg to fprintf - rdx
= argv[i]
call fprintf ; write entry to file
...
section .rodata
fmtPrint db "%s", LF, EOL
```

2. Modify sum.asm to calcFile.asm. It should read the file calc.txt (see above). It should display each entry, convert it to a double, and sum all of the entries. Use the techniques shown in sum.asm to convert each string to a floating point value.
3. Modify sum.asm to calcFile2.asm. It should read calc.txt using the glibc function fscanf.
4. Why is fprintf a varadic function?

CHAPTER 9

The commaSeparate Utility

The value returned by the factorial program was hard to read. We now present a utility which takes a long integer n and returns a string representing n with commas inserted into the correct positions. Table 9-1 shows the algorithm. We use the temporary register r10 to keep track of whether a non-zero quotient has been found. Nowhere else in the program is r10 used, so there is no difficulty in using it as a temporary variable. This means that your program doesn't need to save and restore r10. Listing 9-1 shows the current incarnation of our ever changing macro.inc. Listing 9-2 shows the utility commaSeparate.asm.

Table 9-1. *commaSeparate Utility*

Division	Action
n / 1 QUINTILLION	if quotient > 0, write 3 digits of quotient followed by comma*
remainder / 1 QUADRILLION	if quotient > 0, write 3 digits of quotient followed by comma*
remainder / 1 TRILLION	if quotient > 0, write 3 digits of quotient followed by comma*
remainder / 1 BILLION	if quotient > 0, write 3 digits of quotient followed by comma*
remainder / 1MILLION	if quotient > 0, write 3 digits of quotient followed by comma*
remainder / 1THOUSAND	if quotient > 0, write 3 digits of quotient followed by comma*
remainder	if quotient > 0, write 3 digits of quotient*

**In Table 9-1, we don't write until the first nonzero quotient has been written.*

J. Schwartzman, *Assembly Language Reimagined*, https://doi.org/10.1007/979-8-8688-1724-3_9

Listing 9-1. macro.inc

```
;=============================================================================
; macro.inc - assembly language macros
; John Schwartzman, Forte Systems, Inc.
; 05/26/2023
;=============================================================================
;============================= DEFINE MACRO ==============================
%macro      zero    1
    xor     %1, %1
%endmacro

;============================= DEFINE MACRO ==============================
%macro prologue 0                  ;=== prologue macro takes 0 arguments ===
      push      rbp                ; set up stack frame
      mov       rbp, rsp           ; set up stack frame - stack now aligned
%endmacro

;============================= DEFINE MACRO ==============================
%macro epilogue 0                  ;=== epilogue macro takes 0 arguments ===
      leave                        ; restore rbp and rsp
      ret                          ; return from function
%endmacro

;=============================================================================
```

Listing 9-2. commaSeparate.asm

```
;=============================================================================
; commaSeparate.asm
; John Schwartzman, Forte Systems, Inc.
; 05/26/2023
; Linux x86_64
; useful utility for writing a long as a comma separated string
```

```
;
;========================= CONSTANT DEFINITIONS ======================
LF              equ       10               ; ASCII linefeed character
EOL             equ        0               ; end of line character
VAR_SIZE        equ        8               ; number of bytes in a variable
NUM_VAR         equ        2               ; number local var (round up to even num)
BUFF_SIZE       equ       32               ; string destination
TEN             equ       10
HUNDRED         equ      100
THOUSAND        equ     1000
MILLION         equ     THOUSAND * THOUSAND
BILLION         equ     THOUSAND * MILLION
TRILLION        equ     THOUSAND * BILLION
QUADRILLION     equ     THOUSAND * TRILLION
QUINTILLION     equ     THOUSAND * QUADRILLION

; NOTE: SEXTILLION equ THOUSAND * QUINTILLION doesn't fit in a 64 bit field

%include "macro.asm"

;============================ DEFINE MACRO ===========================
%macro  writePowerOfTenToThird    1  ; power is the divisor
        zero    rdx
        mov     rax, n               ; get n; n (rdx:rax) is the dividend
        mov     rcx, %1              ; %1 = power
        div     rcx                  ; rax = power / n, rdx = remainder
        mov     rdi, rax             ; rax = quotient
        mov     n, rdx               ; save remainder (what's left of n)
        call    writeThreeDigits     ; write quotient
        call    writeComma           ; write comma if bFound != ZERO
%endmacro

```

```
;============================ DEFINE MACRO ============================
%macro  writeUnits  0
     mov     rdi, n                   ; get what's left of n
     call    writeThreeDigits
     call    writeEOL
%endmacro

;====================== DEFINE LOCAL VARIABLES ======================
%define      n     qword [rsp + VAR_SIZE * (NUM_VAR - 2)]     ; rsp + 0

;=========================== CODE SECTION ============================
section      .text                 ;=========== CODE SECTION ===========

%ifndef __MAIN__                   ;======== BUILD WITHOUT MAIN ========

global       commaSeparate         ; tell linker about exports

%else                              ;========= BUILD WITH MAIN ==========

global       main                  ; tell linker about exports
extern       printf, scanf         ; tell assembler/linker about externals

;========================== MAIN FUNCTION ============================
main:
     prologue
     sub     rsp, NUM_VAR * VAR_SIZE ; make space for n

     lea     rdi, [promptFormat]      ; 1st arg to printf
     zero    rax                      ; printf has no floating point args
     call    printf                   ; prompt user

     lea     rdi, [scanfFormat]       ; 1st arg to scanf
     lea     rsi, n                   ; 2nd arg to scanf
```

```
    zero    rax                         ; scanf has no floating point args
    call    scanf                       ; get n

    mov     rdi, n                      ; n is the long we want to separate
    lea     rsi, [outputBuf]            ; destination
    call    commaSeparate               ; return pointer to outputBuf in rax

    lea     rdi, [outputFinal]
    lea     rsi, [outputBuf]
    zero    rax
    call    printf                      ; write output

    zero    rax                         ; return 0 for success
    epilogue

%endif  ;================== BUILD WITH MAIN ========================

;======================== EXPORTED FUNCTION ========================
commaSeparate:                         ; param rdi = long int - rsi => outputBuf
    prologue
    sub     rsp, NUM_VAR * VAR_SIZE ; make space for n
    zero    r10                         ; this function uses r10 as bQuotientFound

    mov     n, rdi                      ; get/save parameter (n)
    or      rdi, rdi                    ; n == 0 ?
    jnz     .continue                   ; jump if no
    call    writeZero                   ; special case to write n = 0
    jmp     fin

.continue:
    writePowerOfTenToThird QUINTILLION  ; n / 1 QUINTILLION
    writePowerOfTenToThird QUADRILLION  ; n / 1 QUADRILLION
    writePowerOfTenToThird TRILLION     ; n / 1 TRILLION
```

```
      writePowerOfTenToThird BILLION      ; n / 1 BILLION
      writePowerOfTenToThird MILLION      ; n / 1 MILLION
      writePowerOfTenToThird THOUSAND     ; n / 1000
      writeUnits                          ; n / 1

fin:
      zero    rax                         ; return EXIT_SUCCESS
      epilogue

;========================= LOCAL FUNCTION ============================
writeThreeDigits:                     ; parameter: rdi = any int from
                                        0 to 999
      prologue

      mov     rax, rdi
      zero    rdx
      mov     rcx, HUNDRED
      div     rcx                      ; rax = number of hundreds
      call    writeNTmp                ; write hundreds

      mov     rax, rdx                ; process remainder (tens and ones)
      zero    rdx
      mov     rcx, TEN
      div     rcx                      ; rax = number of tens
      call    writeNTmp                ; write tens

      mov     rax, rdx                 ; rax = number of ones
      call    writeNTmp                ; write ones

      epilogue

;====================== LOCAL LEAF FUNCTION ==========================
writeComma:                           ; no arguments
      or      r10, r10                ; bQuotientFound?
      jz      .noWrite                ; jump if no
```

```
    mov     al, ','
    mov     [rsi], al                   ; write comma into output buffer
    inc     rsi

.noWrite:
    ret

;========================= LOCAL LEAF FUNCTION ======================
writeNTmp    ; rax = (0-9), rsi => outputBuf
    or      al, al                      ; al == 0 ?
    jnz     .continue                   ; jump if no
    or      r10, r10                    ; bQuotientFound?
    jz     .fin                         ; jump of no - don't write '0'

.continue:
    inc     r10                         ; ++bQuotientFound
    add     al, '0'                     ; convert to char
    mov     [rsi], al                   ; write char
    inc     rsi                         ; increment write pointer

.fin:
    ret

;======================== LOCAL LEAF FUNCTION =======================
writeZero:                              ; rax = n (0)
    add     al, '0'                     ; convert to char
    mov     [rsi], al                   ; write char
    inc      rsi                        ; increment write pointer
                                        ; fall through into writeEOL

;======================== LOCAL LEAF FUNCTION =======================
writeEOL:
    xor     al, al
    mov     [rsi], al                   ; write a zero to end the string
    ret

```

```
;==========================================================================

%ifdef __MAIN__                        ; no data sections if no main
;======================= UNINITIALIZED DATA SECTION ===================
section      .bss
outputBuf    resb       BUFF_SIZE

;===================== READ-ONLY DATA SECTION ========================
section            .rodata
scanfFormat        db            "%ld", EOL
promptFormat       db            LF, "Enter a positive long integer: ", EOL
outputFormat       db            LF, LF, EOL
outputFinal        db            "commaSeparated Value: %s", LF, EOL

;==========================================================================
%endif                                 ; ===== ifdef __MAIN__ =====
```

To build factorial with commaSeparate.asm please type the following:

```
js@suse-tumbleweed-z4:~/Development/asm_x86_64/commaSeparate$ cd ../factorial
js@suse-tumbleweed-z4:~/Development/asm_x86_64/factorial$ make DEF=__COMMA__
##### release __COMMA__ build #####
yasm -f elf64 ../commaSeparate/commaSeparate.asm -o commaSeparate.obj
yasm -D __COMMA__ -f elf64 factorial.asm -o factorial.obj
gcc -z noexecstack factorial.obj commaSeparate.obj -o factorial
gcc -Wall -O3 -z noexecstack -D __COMMA__ factorial.c commaSeparate.obj
js@suse-tumbleweed-z4:~/Development/asm_x86_64/factorial$ ./factorial

Enter a positive integer from 1 to 20: 20
20! = 2432902008176640000
20! = 2,432,902,008,176,640,000
js@suse-tumbleweed-z4:~/Development/asm_x86_64/factorial$ ./a.out

Enter a positive integer less than or equal to 20: 20
```

```
20! = 2432902008176640000
20! = 2,432,902,008,176,640,000
```

It's really much easier to read a large number when it's comma separated! To make sure you follow the code, you might want to make the debug version and run it through the debugger:

```
$ make DEF=__COMMA__ debug
$ ddd factorial
```

Activities

1. Modify Makefile so that it copies factorial to /usr/local/bin.
2. Modify Makefile again, so that it has an install target which will copy factorial to /usr/local/bin.
3. Verify that "make install" works properly.
4. Modify Makefile so that it links factorial to commaSeparate.
5. Does commaSeparate make the output of factorial easier to read?

CHAPTER 10

The hhmmss Utility Program

The hhmmss utility program displays a long integer, number of Seconds, in hhmmss string format. It can display a maximum value of 99:59:59. Table 10-1 shows the algorithm and Listing 10-2 shows the c calling program.

Table 10-1. *The hhmmss Algorithm*

Division	Action
number of Seconds / 60 * 60	write 2 digits of quotient followed by a colon (hours)
remainder / 60	write 2 digits of quotient followed by a colon (minutes)
remainder	write 2 digits of quotient (seconds)

```
//////////////////////////////////////////////////////////////////////////////
// hhmmss.c
// John Schwartzman, Forte Systems, Inc.
// 05/28/2023
// x86_64
//////////////////////////////////////////////////////////////////////////////
#include <time.h>
#include <stdio.h> // declaration of printf
#include <stdlib.h> // defines EXIT_SUCCESS

int toHHMMSS(long nSeconds, char* buffer); // declaration of asm function

int main(void)
```


J. Schwartzman, *Assembly Language Reimagined*, https://doi.org/10.1007/979-8-8688-1724-3_10

```
{
        char buffer[32];
        time_t t = time(NULL);
        struct tm lt = *localtime(&t);
        long nSeconds = lt.tm_hour * 60 * 60 + lt.tm_min * 60 + lt.tm_sec;
        int nRetVal = toHHMMSS(nSeconds, buffer); // call toHHMMSS
        printf("\nThe current time is: %s\n", buffer);

        nSeconds = 99 * 60 * 60 + lt.tm_min * 60 + lt.tm_sec;
        nRetVal = toHHMMSS(nSeconds, buffer);
        printf("Elapsed time: %s\n\n", buffer);
        return nRetVal;
}
```

Listing 10-1. hhmmss.asm

```
;==============================================================================
; hhmmss.asm
; John Schwartzman, Forte Systems, Inc.
; 05/26/2023
; linux x86_64
; Useful utility for converting elapsed time in seconds into hh:mm:ss
;
;========================= CONSTANT DEFINITIONS =======================
VAR_SIZE       equu      8          ; number of bytes in a variable
NUM_VAR        equ       2          ; number local var (round up to even num)
LF             equ      10          ; ASCII linefeed character
EOL            equ       0          ; end of line character
ONE            equ       1          ; number 1
TEN            equ      10          ; number 10
SIXTY          equ      60          ; number 60
BUFF_SIZE      equ      32

%include "macro.asm"

```

```
section         .text                       ;======== CODE SECTION ==========

%ifndef __MAIN__                            ;====== BUILD WITHOUT MAIN ======

global          toHHMMSS                    ; tell linker about export

%else                                       ;======= BUILD WITH MAIN =======

global      main                            ; tell linker about exports
extern      printf, scanf                   ; tell assembler/linker about externals

;======================= DEFINE LOCAL VARIABLES =======================
%define     n    qword [rsp + VAR_SIZE * (NUM_VAR - 2)]    ; rsp + 0

;========================== MAIN FUNCTION ===========================
main:
     prologue
     sub      rsp, NUM_VAR * VAR_SIZE  ; make space for local variable n

     mov       n, 22 * 60 * 60 + 22 * 60 + 22       ; 22 hours, 22 min, 22 sec

     mov       rdi, n                     ; n is the long we want in hh:mm:ss fmt
     lea       rsi, [outputBuf]           ; destination
     call   toHHMMSS                      ; return pointer to outputBuf in rax

     lea       rdi, [outputFinal]
     mov       rsi, n
     lea       rdx, [outputBuf]
     zero      rax
     call      printf                     ; write result

     zero      rax
```

```
    epilogue

%endif  ;================= BUILD WITHOUT MAIN ========================

;========================= EXPORTED FUNCTION ========================
toHHMMSS:                           ; param rdi = long int - rsi => outputBuf
    prologue

    mov     rax, rdi                ; rdi = param
    zero    rdx
    mov     rcx, SIXTY * SIXTY
    div     rcx                     ; rax = num hours

    push    rdx                     ; save remainder = num min + num seconds
    mov     rdi, rax
    call    writeTwoDigits          ; write num hours
    call    writeColon
    pop     rax                     ; restore remainder

    mov     rcx, SIXTY
    zero    rdx
    div     rcx                     ; rax = num minutes

    push    rdx                     ; save remainder = num seconds
    mov     rdi, rax
    call    writeTwoDigits          ; write num minutes
    call    writeColon
    pop     rdi                     ; restore remainder

    call    writeTwoDigits          ; write num seconds

    zero    rax                     ; return EXIT_SUCCESS
```

```
    epilogue

;========================== LOCAL FUNCTION ============================
writeTwoDigits:                         ; param:  rdi = int 0 through 99
    prologue

    mov     rax, rdi                    ; rax = dividend
    zero    rdx
    mov     rcx, TEN                    ; tens
    div     rcx                         ; rax = number of tens
    call    writeDigit                  ; writes the byte in al

    mov     rax, rdx                    ; rax = remainder = number of ones
    call    writeDigit                  ; writes the byte in al

    epilogue

;======================== LOCAL LEAF FUNCTION ========================
writeDigit:                             ; no parameter; rax = 0-9
    add     al, '0'                     ; convert to char
    mov     [rsi], al                   ; write char
    inc     rsi                         ; increment write pointer
    ret

;======================== LOCAL LEAF FUNCTION ========================
writeColon:                             ; no parameter
    mov     al, ':'
    mov     [rsi], al
    inc     rsi
    ret

;=====================================================================

```

```
%ifdef __MAIN__                                          ; no data sections if no main
;======================= UNINITIALIZED DATA SECTION ==================
section                .bss
outputBuf     resb      BUFF_SIZE

;====================== READ-ONLY DATA SECTION =======================
section      .rodata
outputFinal  db           "prettified Value of %ld: %s", LF, LF, EOL

;=====================================================================
%endif                                                 ; ===== ifdef __MAIN__
```

Makefile demonstrates how we include the main() function when we make hhmmss.

Listing 10-2. Makefile for hhmmss

```
###############################################################################
#
#      Makefile for hhmmss
#       John Schwartzman, Forte Systems, Inc.
#       05/28/2023
#
#      Commands:  make [.release], make .debug, make clean
#                     make DEF=__MAIN__ [.release]
#                     make DEF=__MAIN__ .debug
#
#   Requires:  ../maketest.sh
#
###############################################################################
PROG  := hhmmss
SHELL := /bin/bash

ifeq ($(DEF), __MAIN__)      ##### STAND ALONE PROGRAM

.release: $(PROG).asm $(PROG).c Makefile
      @source ../maketest.sh && test .release .debug
      yasm -D $(DEF) -f elf64 -o $(PROG).obj $(PROG).asm
```

```
	gcc -Wall -z noexecstack $(PROG).c $(PROG).obj -o $(PROG)

.debug: $(PROG).asm $(PROG).c Makefile
	@source ../maketest.sh && test .debug .release
	yasm -D $(DEF) -f elf64 -g dwarf2 -o $(PROG).obj $(PROG).asm
	gcc -g -z noexecstack $(PROG).obj -o $(PROG)

else      ############ $(PROG).c calls $(PROG).obj #####################

.release: $(PROG).c $(PROG).asm Makefile
	@source ../maketest.sh && test .release .debug

	yasm -f elf64 -o $(PROG).obj $(PROG).asm
	gcc -Wall -z noexecstack $(PROG).c $(PROG).obj -o $(PROG)

.debug: $(PROG).c $(PROG).asm Makefile
	@source ../maketest.sh && test .debug .release
	yasm -f elf64 -g dwarf2 -o $(PROG).obj $(PROG).asm
	gcc -g -z noexecstack $(PROG).c $(PROG).obj -o $(PROG)
endif     ##############################################################

clean:
	rm -f $(PROG) $(PROG).obj $(PROG).lst .debug .release
#######################################################################
```

This utility is useful when you want to display a time given in number_of_seconds as hours, minutes, and seconds. Please build and execute hhmmss.

```
js@suse-tumbleweed-z4:~/Development/asm_x86_64/factorial$ cd ../hhmmss
js@suse-tumbleweed-z4:~/Development/asm_x86_64/hhmmss$ make
yasm -f elf64 -o hhmmss.obj hhmmss.asm
gcc -Wall -z noexecstack hhmmss.c hhmmss.obj -o hhmmss
js@suse-tumbleweed-z4:~/Development/asm_x86_64/hhmmss$ ./hhmmss

The current time is: 20:03:01
Elapsed time: 99:03:01
```

Activities

1. hhmmss.asm contains a bug. It writes some junk characters after a time. Fix the bug.
2. Why do we zero rdx in line 91 of hhmmss.asm (Listing 10-1)?
3. Modify hhmmss so that it can measure an elapsed time of 999 hours.
4. Modify Makefile so that it copies hhmmss to /usr/local/bin.
5. Why do we copy hhmmss to /usr/local/bin?

CHAPTER 11

Creating and Using a Shared Library

We've already used one shared library, glibc.

We're now going to take two utility programs and turn them into a single shared library. Shared libraries are useful for distributing a program. Multiple programs can use the shared library simultaneously. Shared libraries are also a great way to distribute updates to a program.

The linker can find the shared libraries associated with a program. The programs that we want to distribute are commaSeparate.asm and hhmmss.asm. We will link the shared library, libNumUtility.so, with our test programs factorial.c and hhmmss.c. The Makefile for this process is shown in Listing 11-1. Listing 11-2 shows an early version of macro.inc. Listing 11-3 shows our cpp header file, numutility.h. Listing 11-4 shows our calling program factorial.c which contains the function long factorial(int n). Listing 11-5 (hhmmss.cpp) which, in turn, invokes toHHMMSS() in our shared library.

Listing 11-1. Makefile for libNumUtility.so

```
##########################################################################
#       Makefile: for libNumUtility.so
#       John Schwartzman, Forte Systems, Inc.
#       05/28/2023
#
#       Commands:  make [.release]
#                       make DEF=__DEBUG__
#                       make clean
#       Requires:  ../maketest.sh
#
##########################################################################
```


J. Schwartzman, *Assembly Language Reimagined*, https://doi.org/10.1007/979-8-8688-1724-3_11

```
SHELL           := /bin/bash
C_FLAGS         := -Wall -O3 -z noexecstack -fPIC -shared
C_DFLAGS        := -Wall -g -fPIC -shared -z noexecstack
ASM_FLAGS       := -f elf64
ASM_DFLAGS      := -f elf64 -g dwarf2

.PHONY: clean

ifneq ($(DEF), __DEBUG__)      ##### make release #####

.release: Makefile
        $(info ##### release build #####)
        @source ../maketest.sh && test .release .debug
        yasm $(ASM_FLAGS) ../commaSeparate/commaSeparate.asm -o comma
        Separate.obj
        yasm $(ASM_FLAGS) ../hhmmss/hhmmss.asm -o hhmmss.obj
        gcc $(C_FLAGS) commaSeparate.obj hhmmss.obj -o ../../lib/
        libNumUtility.so
        sudo ldconfig -n ../../lib/
        gcc -Wall -O3 hhmmss.c -o hhmmss -L ../../lib -l NumUtility
        gcc -Wall -O3 factorial.c -o factorial -L ../../lib -l NumUtility

else                                          ##### debug #####

.debug: Makefile
        $(info ##### debug build #####)
        @source ../maketest.sh && test .debug .release
        yasm $(ASM_DFLAGS) ../commaSeparate/commaSeparate.asm -o comma
        Separate.obj
        yasm $(ASM_DFLAGS) ../hhmmss/hhmmss.asm -o hhmmss.obj
        gcc $(C_DFLAGS) commaSeparate.obj hhmmss.obj -o ../../lib/
        libNumUtility.so
        sudo ldconfig -n ../../lib/
        gcc -Wall -g hhmmss.c -o hhmmss -L ../../lib -l NumUtility
        gcc -Wall -g factorial.c -o factorial -L ../../lib -l NumUtility

endif

clean:
        rm -f *.obj .debug .release
```

Listing 11-2. An Early Version of macro.inc

```
;==========================================================================
; macro.inc - x86_64 assembly language macros
; John Schwartzman, Forte Systems, Inc.
; 05/18/2023
;==========================================================================
;============================ DEFINE MACRO ================================
%macro      zero    1
    xor     %1, %1
%endmacro

;============================ DEFINE MACRO ================================
%macro prologue     0                   ;=== prologue macro takes 0 arguments ===
    push    rbp                         ; set up stack frame
    mov     rbp, rsp                    ; set up stack frame - stack now aligned
%endmacro

;============================ DEFINE MACRO ================================
%macro epilogue 0                       ; == epilogue macro takes 0 arguments ==
    leave                               ; undo prologue
    ret                                 ; return
%endmacro

;==========================================================================
```

Listing 11-3. numutility.h

```
//////////////////////////////////////////////////////////////////////////
// numutility.h - declarations for the functions in libNumUtility.so
// John Schwartzman, Forte Systems, Inc.
// 12/21/2023
//////////////////////////////////////////////////////////////////////////
```

```
#ifdef __cplusplus
extern "C"
{
#endif  // __cplusplus

int commaSeparate(long n, char* buffer);
int toHHMMSS(long nSeconds, char* buffer);

#ifdef __cplusplus
};
#endif  // __cplusplus
```

Listing 11-4. factorial.c

```
// factorial.c
// John Schwartzman, Forte Systems, Inc.
// 05/27/2023

#include <stdio.h>             // declares printf and scanf
#include "numutility.h"        // declares commaSeparate

#define MAX_INT 20

// recursive function to compute factorial of n
long factorial(int n)
{
    if (n == 1) // base case
    {
        return 1;
    }
    else
    {
        return (n * factorial(n - 1));
    }
}

int main()
```

```
{
    int     n;
    long    fact;
    char    buffer[32];

    do
    {
        printf("\nEnter a positive integer less than or equal to %d: ", MAX_INT);
        scanf("%d", &n);
    }
    while (n < 1 || n > MAX_INT);

    fact = factorial(n);
    printf("%d! = %ld\n", n, fact);

    int nRetVal = commaSeparate(fact, buffer);
    printf("%d! = %s\n\n", n, buffer);
    return nRetVal;
}
```

Listing 11-5. hhmmss.cpp

```
///////////////////////////////////////////////////////////////////////////
// hhmmss.cpp
// John Schwartzman, Forte Systems, Inc.
// 05/27/2023
///////////////////////////////////////////////////////////////////////////
#include <time.h>
#include <stdio.h>          // declaration of printf
#include "numutility.h"     // declares toHHMMSS
#include <iostream>

int main(void)
{
    char buffer[32];
    time_t t = time(NULL);
```

```
    struct tm lt = *localtime(&t);
    long nSeconds = lt.tm_hour * 60 * 60 + lt.tm_min * 60 + lt.tm_sec;

    int nRetVal = toHHMMSS(nSeconds, buffer);    // call toHHMMSS
    printf("\nCurrent time: %s\n", buffer);

    int nDay = 24 * 60 * 60;                     // num hours in a day
    nSeconds = nDay + lt.tm_hour * 60 * 60 + lt.tm_min * 60 + lt.tm_sec;
    nRetVal = toHHMMSS(nSeconds, buffer);        // call toHHMMSS

   std::cout << "Elapsed time: "
             << buffer
             << std::endl;
    return nRetVal;
}
```

Note that when we assemble ../commaSeparate/commaSeparate.asm and ../hhmmss/hhmmss.asm, we do not define __MAIN__. These two files will not have a main(), and they will not have a .data section. That's what we need to make a shared library. We've also included macro.asm in these two programs.

Also note that we've included **numutility.h** in both of our test programs, factorial.c and hhmmss.cpp. Once we build a shared library, it makes sense to define a header file for the users of the shared library so the compiler won't complain about undeclared functions.

So far we've done all our work in C, but you'll notice that hhmmss.cpp is a C++ file, and C++ is used in Makefile to compile our test programs factorial.c and hhmmss.cpp. C++ does name mangling and it would have trouble finding the two functions toHHMMSS() and commaSeparate() if we hadn't declared them both as extern "C". If you're going to use assembly language with both C and C++, be sure to tell your compiler that your assembly language programs are declared extern "C"!

Now let's take a look at the Makefile for this project (Listing 10A). In our ~/.bashrc file, we defined `export LD_LIBRARY_PATH=$LD_LIBRARY_PATH:~/Development/lib.` That gives us a place to put library files that are under development.

After we assemble our two assembly files, we combine them into a library with the command gcc -Wall -O3 -z noexecstack -fPIC -shared commaSeparate.obj hhmmss.obj -o ../../lib/libNumUtility.so (Listing 10A, line 27). In line 28, we copy the library into our

LD_LIBRARY_PATH directory. Finally, in line 29 we invoke sudo ldconfig -n /home/js/Development/lib/. This creates the symbolic links necessary to find the shared library in ~/Development/lib.

When we compile and link hhmmss.c and factorial.c (Listing 10A, lines 30 and 31), we specify the location of the new shared library for them to link to (L ../../lib) since it's not in the standard location. We also specify the name of the library with -l NumUtility. The -l prefixes lib to the name of the library, and adds the suffix .so (shared object). So the lib we link to is named libNumUtility.so and it resides in ~/Development/lib.

Now build and test the library.

```
js@suse-tumbleweed-z4:~/Development/asm_x86_64/makelib$ make
##### release build #####
yasm -f elf64 ../commaSeparate/commaSeparate.asm -o commaSeparate.obj
yasm -f elf64 ../hhmmss/hhmmss.asm -o hhmmss.obj
gcc -Wall -O3 -z noexecstack -fPIC -shared  commaSeparate.obj hhmmss.obj -o
../../lib/libNumUtility.so
sudo ldconfig -n ../../lib/
c++ -Wall -O3 hhmmss.c -o hhmmss -L ../../lib -l NumUtility
c++ -Wall -O3 factorial.c -o factorial -L ../../lib -l NumUtility
js@suse-tumbleweed-z4:~/Development/asm_x86_64/makelib$ ./factorial

Enter a positive integer less than or equal to 20: 20
20! = 2432902008176640000
20! = 2,432,902,008,176,640,000

js@suse-tumbleweed-z4:~/Development/asm_x86_64/makelib$ ./hhmmss

Current time: 13:33:15
Elapsed time: 99:33:15

js@suse-tumbleweed-z4:~/Development/asm_x86_64/makelib$
```

Type 'make DEF=__DEBUG__' if you want to use the library in the debugger.

To see what needs to be loaded when we run factorial, we can use the Linux ldd utility which lists all dependencies.

```
js@suse-tumbleweed-z4:~/Development/asm_x86_64/makelib$ ldd factorial
        linux-vdso.so.1 (0x00007ffe3b371000)
```

```
libNumUtility.so => /home/js/Development/lib/libNumUtility.so
(0x00007f4d13e88000)
libc.so.6 => /lib64/libc.so.6 (0x00007f4d13c70000)
/lib64/ld-linux-x86-64.so.2 (0x00007f4d13e8f000)
```

We see our shared library libNumUtility.so and libc.so.6, which is the C runtime library shared glibc library. Also present are linux-vdso.so.1, a userspace helper library, and ld-linux-x86-64.so.2, which is the runtime loader. These must all be present in order for you to run factorial or hhmmss. We see that libNumUtility.so is a *symbolic link* to /home/js/Development/lib/libNumUtility.so. We see here that that path is our $LD_LIBRARY_PATH variable.

```
js@suse-tumbleweed-z4:~/Development/asm_x86_64/makelib$ echo $LD_
LIBRARY_PATH
:~/Development/lib
```

Activities

1. Verify that Makefile will fail to build our hhmmss.cpp utility program if we don't include numutility.h or if we don't declare our library functions as extern "C" in numutility.h.

2. Write a C or C++ utility program named fibonacciCount.cpp to count up to a nextTerm limit of 100 trillion using the fibonacci sequence. Print each nextTerm right justified in a 20-character field. Your output should look like the lines shown here.

```
js@suse-tumbleweed-z4:~/Development/asm_x86_64/makelib$
./fibonacci
Fibonacci Series:
                   0
                   1
                   1
                   2
                   3
                   5
                   8
```

```
  13
  21
  34
  55
  89
 144
 233
 377
 610
 987
1597
. . .
```

3. Modify Makefile so that it builds your new program in addition to its previous tasks.

4. Add commaSeparate to your program so that it will be easier to read the results. Print each nextTerm right justified in a 20-character field. Link your program to libNumUtility.so to add commaSeparate. Verify that the results are much easier to read.

CHAPTER 12

Sorting an Array of Integers

We've come to the most challenging, and I think, potentially, the most rewarding point in the course. We're going to take an algorithm which has been implemented in the C programming language and convert it into assembly language. This demonstrates how C code can be broken down into a much larger quantity of assembly language instructions. It will also demonstrate exactly what actions are performed by each of the components of a C implementation of a *structured* high-level algorithm.

We're going to take the bubblesort, a slow, O(n^2), implementation of a C algorithm, and convert it into Intel assembly language. It should, at the very least, give you an appreciation of the power of the C compiler. The *order* of the algorithm shows that for every item, n, that we add to the list, the time to execute the algorithm is proportional to n^2. Order increases from constant time, k to n, to n log n, to n^2 ... From this we see that bubblesort is a rather poor-performing algorithm.

Bubblesort takes the first element in a list of elements and compares it to every other element in the list. If any element is less than the first element, then the two elements are swapped. That puts the lowest element in position 0 in the list. We then repeat this procedure for the second element in the list, the third element, up to and including the nth element. In each iteration, we say that the lowest element has bubbled to the top of the list. Hence the name, bubblesort.

The implementation we're using has a slight optimization. It can tell, by the addition of the Boolean variable bSwapped, after a complete iteration through the outer-loop code, whether it has completed sorting the array.

In C, the code looks like this (Listing 12-1):

J. Schwartzman, *Assembly Language Reimagined*, https://doi.org/10.1007/979-8-8688-1724-3_12

Listing 12-1. The Bubblesort Algorithm Implemented in C

```
/////////////////////////////////////////////////////////////////
// bsortInt.c          Bubblesort an array of integers
// John Schwartzman, Forte Systems, Inc.
// 11/21/2023
/////////////////////////////////////////////////////////////////
#include <stdio.h>
#include <stdbool.h>

int    array[] = { 19, 2, 3, 9, 1, 4, 7, 6, 5, 11, 10 };
int    nArraySize  = sizeof(array) / sizeof(array[0]);

void swap(int a, int b)
{
    int temp = array[a];
    array[a] = array[b];
    array[b] = temp;
}

// An optimized version of the bubblesort algorithm
void bSortInt(int nSize)
{
    int i, j;
    bool bSwapped;

    for (i = 0; i < nArraySize - 1;  i++)            // the outer loop
    {
        bSwapped = false;
        for (j = 0; j < nArraySize - i - 1;  j++)  // the inner loop
        {
            if (array[j] > array[j + 1])
            {
                swap(j, j + 1);
                bSwapped = true;
            }
```

```
        }

        // If no elements were swapped by inner loop, then exit this routine.
        if (!bSwapped)
        {
            break;
        }
    }
}

// Function to print array
void printArray(int nSize)
{
    for (int i = 0; i < nArraySize; i++)
    {
        printf("\t%2d\n", array[i]);
    }
}

int main(void)
{
    puts("\nInsertion Sorted Array:");
    printArray(nArraySize);

    bSortInt(nArraySize);

    puts("\nBubblesorted Array:");
    printArray(nArraySize);
    puts("");
    return 0;
}
```

Note that macro.inc has been updated with succeeding programs. Please be sure to include the latest version of macro.inc in your assembly language programs. Make sure that you understand all of the changes to macro.inc.

Now, without looking at bubblesortInt.asm, try your hand at converting Listing 12-1 into x64 assembly language. Compare your solution with mine (Listing 12-2 - bubblesortInt.asm). Does your implementation sort the array of items? Do you have all of the tests in place?

My version of the assembly code looks like this (Listing 12-2):

Listing 12-2. The bubblesort IntegerAlgorithm Implemented in x64 Assembly Language

```
;==============================================================================
; bubblesortInt.asm     - NOTE: Elements to be sorted are 8-byte qwords.
; John Schwartzman, Forte Systems, Inc.
; 11/21/2023
; Linux x86_64
;
;==============================================================================
%include "macro.inc"

global   bubblesortInt                          ; global procedure
extern   getElement, putElement, swap           ; extern procedure
extern   array, nTempi, nTempj                  ; extern data

%define i           qword [rsp +  0]            ; for bubblesortInt
%define j           qword [rsp +  8]
%define nRecords    qword [rsp + 16]
%define bSwapped    qword [rsp + 24]

;============================ CODE SECTION ===================================
section .text

;==============================================================================
bubblesortInt:
      prologue 4
      mov     nRecords, rsi       ; rsi contains nRecords
      mov     i, 0                ; I = j = 0 prepare for 1st iteration of
                                            outer loop
      mov     j, 0
.outerLoop:
      mov     bSwapped, 0         ; change bSwapped flag to clear
```

```
        mov     j, 0                ; and j = 0

.testOuterLoop:
        mov     rax, nRecords
        dec     rax
        cmp     i, rax
        jnl     .fin

.innerLoop:
.testInnerLoop:
        mov     rax, nRecords
        sub     rax, i
        dec     rax
        cmp     j, rax
        jnl     .endInnerLoop

.doInnerLoop:
        mov     rcx, j
        call    getElement          ; get array[j]
        mov     [nTempi], rax

        mov     rcx, j
        inc     rcx
        call    getElement          ; get array[j + 1]
        mov     [nTempj], rax

.if:
        mov     rax, [nTempi]       ; compare array[j] and array[j + 1]
        cmp     rax, [nTempj]       ; signed comparison - jump
                                      (don't swap) if i<=j
        jng     .endif              ; jng => ascending sort / jg =>
                                      descending sort

        mov     r8, j               ; swap array[j] and array[j + 1]
        mov     r9, j
        inc     r9
        call    swap
        mov     bSwapped, 1         ; set bSwapped flag
```

```
.endif:
      inc     j
      jmp     .innerLoop

.endInnerLoop:
.endOuterLoop:
      testop  bSwapped          ; have we swapped during the outer loop?
      jz      .fin              ; jump if no

      inc     i
      jmp     .outerLoop

.fin:
      epilogue

;==========================================================================
```

Now, examine my version of bubblesortInt.asm.

Notice the way in which we've used the nomenclature of the C program comments to create the labels of the assembly language routine. For example, note the labels .innerLoop, .testInnerLoop, .doInnerLoop, .if, .endif, and .endInnerLoop. Remember that labels that begin with "." are related to a corresponding label of the subroutine, so that ".innerLoop:" refers to "bubblesortInt.innerLoop:" and ".endif" refers to "bubblesortInt.endif". Because of this feature, we can reuse a label in different functions of an assembly language program without conflict. The label .next is a perennial favorite destination.

Compile and execute bsort.c and then assemble, link, and execute bsortInt.asm. Makefile automates the process for you. Note that bubblesortInt.obj is linked with bsortInt.obj, bubblesortInt.obj to become the executable file qsortInt. Please notice that each assembly language file includes an updated macro.inc.

Hopefully, both bsortInt and qsortInt produced identical results.

It is critically important that you faithfully interpret the C code as you write the assembly language version of the program. That's harder than it sounds. Assembly language requires a great number of labels and conditional and unconditional jumps. That would never be tolerated in a high-level language today, but it's *de rigueur* (a strict requirement) in assembly language!

In many cases, you need to perform a conditional jump based on the opposite condition to that shown in a high-level language. Intel has made things a little easier for you by providing mnemonics for opposite conditions. For example, suppose that you need to provide for the condition where nTempi is not less than or equal to nTempj. Well, less than or equal to has the mnemonic jle (jump if less than or equal to). We need to address the condition where nTempi is **not** less than or equal to nTempj. We simply use the mnemonic jnle (jump if **not** less than or equal to). An example from bubblesortInt.asm illustrates this. We jump if nTempi is not greater than nTempj by using the mnemonic jng .endif. We fall through to the code starting with mov r8, j and perform the swap if nTempi is greater than or equal to nTempj. All this makes it a lot easier to interpret the flags in the rflags register.

```
.if:
        mov     rax, [nTempi]       ; compare array[j] and array[j + 1]
        cmp     rax, [nTempj]       ; signed comparison - jump (don't swap)
                                      if i <= j
        jng     .endif              ; jng => ascending sort / use jg =>
                                      descending sort

        mov     r8, j               ; swap array[j] and array[j + 1]
        mov     r9, j
        inc     r9
        call    swap
        mov     bSwapped, 1         ; set bSwapped flag
.endif:
        inc     j
        jmp     .innerLoop
```

The recursive quicksort algorithm, O(n log n), is faster than bubblesort, O(n^2). Try to implement the quicksort algorithm by assembling your own version of quicksortInt.asm (see qsortInt.c - Listing 12-3). How does your result compare to quicksortInt.asm (Listing 12-4)? If you're interested in history, quicksort was written in 1959 by British computer scientist Tony Hoare and published in 1961.[5]

Writing well-performing assembly language requires a lot of practice! How does your code compare to quicksortInt.asm? Have you discovered all of the initializations and tests that go into a structured language for loop? It looks so simple in C; it's not until we attempt to create an assembly language equivalent that we begin to understand the strength of high-level structured language statements.

We have steadily expanded and modified the macro.inc file that is included by all of the .asm programs. The archives contain many different versions of macro.inc. Please make sure that you always include the latest version of macro.inc in your .asm files. This will be the version of macro.inc that is included in each working directory.

Before looking at quicksortInt.asm, try your hand at converting qsortInt.c – Listing 12-3 – into assembly language. How does your program compare with quicksortInt.asm? Does it correctly sort the array of items?

Listing 12-3. The Quicksort Algorithm for Sorting Integers, Implemented in C

```
////////////////////////////////////////////////////////////////
// qsortInt.c
// John Schwartzman, Forte Systems, Inc.
// 11/21/2023
////////////////////////////////////////////////////////////////
#include<stdio.h>

    int array[] = { 19, 2, 3, 9, 1, 4, 7, 6, 5, 11, 10 };

    void quicksort(int nLow, int nHigh)
    {
        int i, j, pivot, temp;

        if (nLow < nHigh)
        {
            pivot = nLow;
            i = nLow;
            j = nHigh;

            while (i < j)
            {
                while(array[i] <= array[pivot] && i < nHigh)
                {
```

```
                    i++;
                }

                while (array[j] > array[pivot])
                {
                    j--;
                }

                if(i < j)
                {
                    temp = array[i];
                    array[i] = array[j];
                    array[j] = temp;
                }
            }

            temp = array[pivot];
            array[pivot] = array[j];
            array[j] = temp;
            quicksort(nLow, j - 1);
            quicksort(j + 1, nHigh);
        }
}

int main(void)
{
        int i, nCount = 11;

        puts("\nInsertion Sorted Array:");
        for(i = 0; i < nCount; i++)
        {
            printf("\t%2d\n", array[i]);
        }

        quicksort(0, nCount - 1);

        puts("\nQuicksort Sorted Array:");
        for(i = 0; i < nCount; i++)
```

```
        {
            printf("\t%2d\n", array[i]);
        }
        puts("");
        return 0;
    }
```

Listing 12-4. The Quicksort Algorithm Implemented in x64 Assembly Language

```
;==========================================================================
; quicksortInt.asm      - NOTE: elements to be sorted are integers.
; John Schwartzman, Forte Systems, Inc.
; 11/11/2023
; Linux x86_64
;
;==========================================================================
ELEMENT_SIZE      equu         8

%include "macro.inc"

global      quicksortInt            ; global procedures
extern      array                   ; extern data
extern      getElement, swap

%define nLow      qword [rsp +  0]  ; for quicksortInt
%define nHigh     qword [rsp +  8]
%define I         qword [rsp + 16]
%define j         qword [rsp + 24]
%define nPivot    qword [rsp + 32]
;========================== CODE SECTION ==================================
section.text

;==========================================================================
quicksortInt:
    prologue 6

    mov     nLow, rdi
    mov     nHigh, rsi
```

```
        mov     i, rdi
        mov     j, rsi
        mov     nPivot, rdi             ; nPivot = nLow

        mov     rax, nLow
        cmp     rax, nHigh
        jnl     .fin
.outerWhile:                            ; while (i < j)
        mov     rax, i
        cmp     rax, j
        jnl     .doSwap

.firstInnerWhile:
        mov     rax, i                  ; if i ! lt nHigh, get out
        cmp     rax, nHigh
        jnl     .endFirstInnerWhile

        mov     rcx, i
        call    getElement              ; get array[i]
        mov     rsi, rax

        mov     rcx, nPivot             ; get array[nPivot]
        call    getElement

        cmp     rsi, rax                ; if array[i] ! lte
array[nPivot], get out
        jnle    .endFirstInnerWhile

        inc     i
        jmp     .firstInnerWhile        ; do another iteration

.endFirstInnerWhile:
.secondInnerWhile:
        mov     rcx, j
        call    getElement
        mov     rsi, rax

        mov     rcx, nPivot
        call    getElement
```

```
        cmp     rsi, rax
        jng     .endSecondInnerWhile

        dec     j
        jmp     .secondInnerWhile

.endSecondInnerWhile:
.if:
        mov     rax, j
        cmp     i, rax
        jnl     .endif

        mov     r8, i
        mov     r9, j
        call    swap

.endif:
        jmp     .outerWhile

.doSwap:
        mov     r8, nPivot          ; exchange array[nPivot] and array[j]
        mov     r9, j
        call    swap

.firstRecursiveCall:
        mov     rdi, nLow
        mov     rsi, j
        dec     rsi
        call    quicksortInt        ; quicksortInt(nLow, j - 1)

.secondRecursiveCall:
        mov     rdi, j
        inc     rdi
        mov     rsi, nHigh
        call    quicksortInt        ; quicksortInt(j + 1, nHigh)

.fin:
        epilogue

;==========================================================================
```

Activities

1. Create a file sortInt.asm that sorts an array of integers. Set a flag on the command line that tells sortInt whether and how to sort its output. You could do something like

   ```
   sortInt -q
   ```

   where -q means quicksort and -b means bubblesort.

   No argument would make sortInt display the information in insertion sorted order. Refer to Chapter 4 if you need a refresher on passing arguments to an assembly language program. A wrong flag or conflicting flags should cause the program to print a USAGE statement and exit. The sortInt program should return EXIT_SUCCESS (0) or EXIT_FAILURE (1). These equates can be found in macro.inc.

2. Execute sortInt from a shell script. The shell script should report the value returned by the sortInt executable.
3. Modify sortInt so that it obtains 100 random numbers and sorts them. Display the array before and after sorting.
4. Modify sortInt so that it searches for a specific number in a sorted array. Continuously divide the list in half until you find (or don't find) the number.
5. Modify bubblesortInt.asm to sort in descending order.
6. Modify quicksortInt to sort in descending order.
7. The program shown below is another C implementation of Quicksort for integers. Verify that qsortInt.c works and then convert it to qsortPartInt.asm. Build, run, and test your program. Modify Makefile so that it will build your executable.

   ```
   // qsortPartInt.c

   #include <stdio.h>                  // for printf
   #include <stdlib.h>                 // for EXIT_SUCCESS

   int array[] = { 10, 7, 8, 9, 1, 5, 13, 11, 0 };
   ```

```
int nArraySize = sizeof(arr) / sizeof(arr[0]);

void swap(int i, int j)
{
    int nTemp = array[i];
    array[i] = array[j];
    array[j] = nTemp;
}

int partition(int nLow, int nHigh)
{
    int nPivot = array[nHigh];
    int i = nLow - 1;

    for(int j = nLow; j < nHigh; j++)
    {
        //If current element is smaller than the pivot
          if(array[j] < pPivot)
          {
                //Increment index of smaller element
                i++;
                swap(i, j);
          }
    }

    swap(i + 1, nHigh);
    return i + 1;
}

void quickSort(int nLow, int nHigh)
{
    // when nLow is less than nHigh
    if(nLow < nHigh)
    {
          int nPivot = partition(nLow, nHigh);

          //Recursive Calls to quickSort
          //smaller element than pivot goes left and
```

```
            //higher element goes right
            quickSort(nLow, nPivot - 1);
            quickSort(nPivot + 1, nHigh);
        }
}

int main(void)
{
    printf("\nInsertion Sorted Array:\n");
    for(int i = 0; i < nArraySize; i++)
    {
        printf("\t%2d\n", arr[i]);
    }

    quickSort(0, nArraySize - 1);

    printf("\nQuicksorted Array:\n");
    for(int i = 0; i < nArraySize; i++)
    {
        printf("\t%2d\n", arr[i]);
    }

    puts("");       // print blank line
    return EXIT_SUCCESS;
}
```

CHAPTER 13

Sorting an Array of Strings

It's time to spread your wings a little bit. We're now going to sort an array of C strings. These are ASCIIZ character representations of C text strings. Whereas an integer takes up a single qbyte (8-bytes or 64 bits) of memory, each C string takes up one byte for each character of the string, followed by a single byte containing zero as a delimiter. A 64-byte string can hold 63 characters plus the ending zero byte. So, it takes 512 bytes of memory (64 * 8) to hold a 64-character C string.

Figure 13-1 shows a C string implementation of the bubblesort algorithm and Figure 13-2 shows the conversion of Figure 13-1 into x64 assembly language.

Note that the instruction strcmp is a glibc function that compares each character in the source and destination strings until it finds a difference. The strcmp function places its less-than-zero, equal-to-zero, greater-than-zero result in the 32-bit eax register. It's up to you to test eax and set the rflags register accordingly. We do that in the strcmp macro instruction.

```
%macro strcmp 0                     ; 0-argument macro instruction
        call    strcmp              ; strcmp changes rax, test checks flags
        test    eax, eax            ; AND eax to itself in order to set rflage
%endmacro

%macro strcmp 2                     ; 2-argument macro instruction
        lea        rdi, %1
        lea        rsi, %2
        strcmp                      ; invoke 0-argument strcmp macro
instruction
%endmacro
```


J. Schwartzman, *Assembly Language Reimagined*, https://doi.org/10.1007/979-8-8688-1724-3_13

Observe that the strcmp macro instruction has two forms. If we've already populated the rdi and rsi registers, then we call the zero-argument version. The zero-argument macro ANDs eax with itself and sets the rflags register accordingly.

If we want to make assembly look more like a high-level language, we can call the two-argument form of the macro instruction strcmp [pTempi], [pTempj], as shown in line 47 of quicksortStr.asm (Listing 13-2). This looks more like int strcmp(char* str1, char* str2).

The macro loads the effective address of the local variable pTempi into rdi and loads the effective address of the local variable pTempj into rsi and then invokes the 0-argument version of the macro instruction, which calls glibc's strcmp and then performs the test eax, eax which has the effect of setting the rflags register. Once rflags has been altered, we can call jle .endWhile1 in line 56, which is the same as jng (Jump if Not Greater than zero).

Listing 13-1. bsortStr.c

```
//////////////////////////////////////////////////////////////////////
// bsortStr.c
// John Schwartzman, Forte Systems, Inc.
// 11/21/2023
//////////////////////////////////////////////////////////////////////
#include <stdio.h>
#include <stdlib.h>      // for EXIT_SUCCESS
#include <string.h>      // for strcmp
#include <stdbool.h>     // for bool, true, false

// global variables
char* array[] =
{
        "Fred Flintstone",
        "Barney Rubble",
        "Wilma Flintstone",
        "Betty Rubble",
        "Dino the Dinosaur",
        "Fido the Dogasauraus",
        "Rasputin the Mystic",
        "Jack the Giant Killer",
```

```
        "Homer the Odyssey",
        "Warner the Brother #2",
        "Warner the Brother #1"
};
int nArraySize = sizeof array / sizeof array[0];

void swap(int a, int b)
{
        char* pTemp = array[a];
        array[a] = array[b];
        array[b] = pTemp;
}

void bsortStr(int nSize)
{
        bool bSwapped;

        for (int i = 0; i < (nSize - 1); i++)                    // outer
                                                                 for loop
        {
                bSwapped = false;
                for (int j = 0; j < (nSize - i - 1); j++)       // inner
                                                                for loop
                {
                        if (strcmp(array[j], array[j + 1]) > 0)
                        {
                                swap(j, j + 1);
                                bSwapped = true;
                        }
                }
                if (!bSwapped)
                {
                        return;
                }
        }
}
```

```
int main(void)
{
        puts("\nStrings in Insertion Sorted Order:");
        for (int i = 0; i < nArraySize; i++)
        {
                printf("\t%s\n", array[i]);
        }

        bsortStr(nArraySize);

        puts("\nStrings in Bubblesorted Order:");
        for (int i = 0; i < nArraySize; i++)
        {
                printf("\t%s\n", array[i]);
        }
        puts("");
   return EXIT_SUCCESS;
}
```

Listing 13-2. bubblesortStr.asm

```
;============================================================================
; bubblesortStr.asm     - NOTE: Elements to be sorted are strings.
; John Schwartzman, Forte Systems, Inc.
; 11/20/2023
; Linux x86_64
;
;============================================================================
%include "macro.inc"

global      bubblesortStr                           ; global procedure
extern      getElement, swap                        ; external proccedures
extern      array, pTemp, pTempi, pTempj            ; external data

%define i               qword [rsp +  0]            ; for BubblesortStr
%define j               qword [rsp +  8]
%define bSwapped        qword [rsp + 16]
```

```
%define nRecords        qword [rsp + 24]

;======================== CODE SECTION ===========================
section        .text

;==================================================================
bubblesortStr:
     prologue 4
     mov       nRecords, rsi                         ; rdi contains nRecords
     mov       j, rdi                                ; j = 0 prepare for .doWhileLoop

.doWhileLoop:
.initOuterForLoop:                                   ; j goes from 0 to nRecords - 1
     mov       bSwapped, false                       ; bSwapped = false
     mov       j, 0

.outerForLoop:
.initInnerForLoop:                                   ; i goes from j + 1 to nRecords
     mov       rax, j
     inc       rax
     mov       i, rax                                ; i = j + 1

.innerForLoop:
     mov       rcx, i
     lea       rdi, [pTempi]
     call      getElement                            ; pTempi now contains array[i]

     mov       rcx, j
     lea       rdi, [pTempj]
     call      getElement                            ; pTempj now contains array[j]
```

```

    strcmp [pTempi], [pTempj]                      ; compare pArray[i] and pArray[j]
    jnl     .endInnerForLoop

    mov     r8, i
    mov     r9, j
    call    swap
    mov     bSwapped, true

.endInnerForLoop:
    inc     i
    mov     rax, i
    cmp     rax, nRecords
    jl      .innerForLoop

.endOuterForLoop:
    mov     rax, nRecords
    dec     rax
    inc     j
    cmp     j, rax                                 ; is j too large?
    jle     .outerForLoop                          ; jump if no

.endDoWhileLoop:
    mov     rax, bSwapped
    test    rax, rax
    jz      .fin                                   ; get out if !bSwapped
    jmp     .initOuterForLoop

.fin:
    epilogue

;=========================================================================
```

Listing 13-3. The Quicksort Algorithm Implemented in C

```
////////////////////////////////////////////////////////////////
// qsortStr.c      C implementation of the Quicksort algorithm
//                 for strings.
// John Schwartzman, Forte Systems, Inc.
// 11/21/2023
////////////////////////////////////////////////////////////////
#include <stdio.h>
#include <string.h>

extern int main(void);
extern char* array[];

void qsort(int nLow, int nHigh);

char* array[] = {
                  "Fred Flintstone",
                  "Barney Rubble",
                  "Wilma Flintstone",
                  "Dino the Dinasaur",
                  "Silvester",
                  "Rutabaga",
                  "Betty Rubble",
                  "Fido the Dogasaurus",
                  "Warner the Brother #2",
                  "Warner the Brother #1"
                };

int nArrayCount = sizeof array / sizeof array[0];

void qsort(int nLow, int nHigh)
{
   int i, j, nPivot;
   char* temp;

   if (nLow < nHigh)
   {
      nPivot = nLow;
```

```
      i = nLow;
      j = nHigh;

      while(i < j)
      {
         while (strcmp(array[i], array[nPivot]) < 0 && i < nHigh)
         {
            i++;
         }
         while (strcmp(array[j], array[nPivot]) > 0)
         {
            j--;
         }
         if (i < j)
         {
            temp = array[i];          // swap array[i] and array[j]
            array[i] = array[j];
            array[j] = temp;
         }
      }

      temp = array[nPivot];           // swap array[nPivot] and array[j]
      array[nPivot] = array[j];
      array[j] = temp;
      qsort(nLow, j - 1);
      qsort(j + 1, nHigh);
   }
}

int main(void)
{
   int i;                                         ; index variable

   puts("\nInsertion Sorted Array:");
   for(i = 0; i < nArrayCount; i++)               ; print the unsorted array
   {
      printf("\t%s\n", array[i]);
```

```
    }

    qsort(0, nArrayCount - 1);                    ; sort the array

    puts("\nQuicksort Sorted Array:");
    for (i = 0; i < nArrayCount; i++) ; print the sorted array
    {
       printf("\t%s\n", array[i]);
    }
    puts("");
    return EXIT_SUCCESS;
}
```

Listing 13-4. The Quicksort Algorithm Implemented in x64 Assembly Language

```
;======================================================================
; quicksortStr.asm - NOTE: elements to be sorted are strings.
; John Schwartzman, Forte Systems, Inc.
; 10/31/2023
; Linux x86_64
;
;======================================================================
%include "macro.inc"

global      quicksortStr                        ; global procedures
extern      getElement, swap                    ; external proccedures
extern      array, pTempi, pTempj               ; external data

%define nLow             qword [rsp +  0]       ; for QuicksortStr
%define nHigh            qword [rsp +  8]
%define nPivot           qword [rsp + 16]
%define i                qword [rsp + 24]
%define j                qword [rsp + 32]

```

```
;========================== CODE SECTION =============================
section       .text

;=====================================================================
quicksortStr:
     prologue 6
     mov      nLow, rdi
     mov      nPivot, rdi
     mov      nHigh, rsi                   ; nHigh = nRecords - 1

.firstIf:
     cmp      rdi, rsi
     jnl      .fin

     mov      nPivot, rdi                  ; nPivot = nLow
     mov      i, rdi                       ; i = nLow
     mov      j, rsi                       ; j = nHigh = nRecords - 1

.outerWhile:
     mov      rax, i
     cmp      rax, j
     jnl      .endOuterWhile

.while1:
     mov      rax, i
     cmp      rax, nHigh                   ; i < nHigh is 1st part of the AND
     jnl      .endWhile1

     mov      rcx, i
     lea      rdi, [pTempi]
     call     getElement

     mov      rcx, nPivot
     lea      rdi, [pTempj]
```

```
    call     getElement

    strcmp [pTempi], [pTempj]          ; pTempi <= pTempj is 2nd part of the AND
    jle      .endWhile1

    inc      i
    jmp      .while1

.endWhile1:
.while2:
    mov      rcx, j
    lea      rdi, [pTempi]
    call     getElement

    mov      rcx, nPivot
    lea      rdi, [pTempj]
    call      getElement

    strcmp [pTempi], [pTempj]      ; this is the only test in while2
    jng      .endWhile2

    dec      j
    jmp      .while2

.endWhile2:
.secondIf:
    mov      rax, i
    cmp      rax, j
    jnl      .endSecondIf

    mov      r8, i
    mov      r9, j
    call     swap
    jmp      .outerWhile
```

```

.endSecondIf:
.doSwap:
     mov      r8, nPivot
     mov      r9, j
     call     swap

.endOuterWhile:
.firstRecursion:
     mov      rdi, nLow
     mov      rsi, j
     dec      rsi
     call     quicksortStr                ; QuicksortStr(nLow, j - 1)

.secondRecursion:
     mov      rdi, j
     inc      rdi
     mov      rsi, nHigh
     call      quicksortStr               ; QuicksortStr(j + 1, nHigh)

.endFirstIf:
.fin:
     epilogue

;================================================================
```

Activities

1. Create a file testStr.asm that sorts an array of strings. Set a flag on the command line that tells testStr whether and how to sort its output. You could do something like this:

   ```
   $ ./testStr -q
   ```

   where -q means quicksort and -b means bubblesort.

No argument would make testStr display the information in insertion sorted order. Refer to Chapter 4 if you need a refresher on passing arguments to an assembly language program. A wrong flag or conflicting flags should cause the program to print a USAGE statement and exit with EXIT_FAILURE. The testStr program should return EXIT_SUCCESS (0) or EXIT_FAILURE (1). These equates can be found in the latest version of macro.inc.

2. Execute testStr from a shell script. The shell script should report the value returned by sortStr.

3. What does the test eax, eax instruction do? Does it change eax? What instructions could you substitute for test?

4. Modify qsortPartitionInt.c so that it will sort C strings. Call the new program qsortPartStr.asm. Build, debug, and test qsortPartStr.asm.

5. Instrument testStr.asm so that it calls bubblesortStr five million times. Get the time when you first call bubblesortStr and get the time when you last call bubblesortStr and subtract the two times. Print the elapsed time.

6. Remove the bSwapped optimization from bubblesortStr and repeat #5. How does the elapsed time compare to #5? Does the bSwapped optimization increase the execution speed? You will see the biggest difference when the list is sorted or partially sorted before calling sort. You can modify testStr.asm so that it reloads the unsorted array before each sort.

7. Call testStr.asm five million times to determine its execution speed.

8. Modify testStr.asm so that it calls quicksortStr five million times and report its elapsed time.

9. Modify testStr.asm so that it calls quicksortPartStr five million times and report its elapsed time.

10. Conduct the elapsed time tests in debug mode and in release mode. How do the times compare?

11. Modify your env.asm program from Chapter 5 so that it sorts the environment variables on property name.

12. Modify env.asm so that it sorts on property value.

13. Add a command line flag to env.asm so that you can control whether it sorts by property name or property value. The default should be property name.

14. Modify Makefile to copy the new program to /usr/local/bin.

15. Modify bubblesortStr.asm so that it sorts in descending order.

16. Modify quicksortStr.asm so that it sorts in descending order.

Searching an Array of Strings

Why did we just spend so much time and energy sorting arrays? It's because finding data in a sorted array is so much faster than finding it in an unsorted array.

It is readily apparent that performing a linear search of a sorted or unsorted array will yield a performance of O(n). To perform a linear search, we start at the beginning of the array and continue moving toward the end of the array until we either find the data we're looking for or we reach the end of the array.

To perform a binary search on a sorted array, however, we search for the data in the first half of the list, and if the data we're searching for is less than the data at the midpoint of the list, we throw away the upper half (or if the data we're searching for is more than the data at the midpoint of the list, we throw away the lower half) of the array. We then continue dividing the lower or upper half of the array into halves again and again until we either find the data or run out of halves in which to search. Because of this halving process, the performance of a binary search on a sorted list is only $O(\log_2 n)$.

So, it seems that we can spend more time inserting into the list or we can spend more time in searching the list. So, which one do you choose? Well, what do you do more often, inserting or searching? If your work is like that of most businesses, inserting a new customer is done far less than accessing that customer's data for adding a new order, or printing a receipt, or printing and mailing a statement, or keeping track of inventory.

So, we've agreed to keep our data in sorted form and to perform a quick search every time we have to access data. The C function shown below performs a binary search of a sorted array (Listing 13-5). Try converting this program to assembly language without looking at the solution (Listing 13-6).

Listing 13-5. A C Function That Performs an Iterative Binary Search on a Sorted Array

```
        int bSearchStr(int nLow, int nHigh, char* pSearchStr)
        {
                int nIndex;

                while (nLow < nHigh)
// while we haven't run out of items to search
                {
                        nIndex = nLow + (nHigh - nLow) / 2

                        if (array[nIndex] == pSearchStr)
                        {
                                return nIndex;             // just right!
                        }

                        if (array[nIndex] < pSearchStr)   // too high
                        {
                                nLow = nIndex + 1;
                        }
                        else
                        {
                                nHigh = nIndex - 1;        // too low
                        }
                }
                return -1;                                 // pSearchStr
                                                           not found
        }
```

Listing 13-6. An Assembly Language Function That Performs an Iterative Binary Search

```
;==============================================================================
; bSearchStr.asm
; John Schwartzman, Forte Systems, Inc.
; Mon Feb 3 04:13:19 PM EST 2025
; Linux x86_64 Linked with arrayTools, bubblesortStr, quicksortStr
; Provides a strcasecmp iterative binary search of a sorted array.
;==============================================================================

%include "macro.inc"

global bSearchStr
extern getElement
extern searchStr, searchStrFmt, searchStrFound, searchStrNotFound, pTemp

%define nLow qword [rsp + 0] ; for bSearchStr
%define nHigh qword [rsp + 8]
%define nIndex qword [rsp + 16]

;========================== CODE SECTION ================================
section .text

;==============================================================================
bSearchStr:
        prologue 4 ; nLow, nHigh

        mov nLow, rdi
        mov nHigh, rsi

.startSearch:
        mov rax, nLow
        cmp rax, nHigh
        jg .notFound ; exit search if (nLow > nHigh)

        mov rax, nHigh
        sub rax, nLow
        sar rax, 1 ; fast integer divide by 2
        mov nIndex, rax
```

```
        mov rax, nLow
        add nIndex, rax ; nIndex = nLow + (nHigh - nLow) / 2

        mov rcx, nIndex
        lea rdi, [pTemp]
        call getElement
        strcasecmp [pTemp], [searchStr]
        jz .found ; array[nIndex] == key

.lessThan: ; array[nIndex] < key
        jg .greaterThan

mov rax, nIndex
inc rax
mov nLow, rax
jmp .startSearch ; loop - try again with different nLow

.greaterThan: ; array[nIndex] > key
        mov rax, nIndex
        dec rax
        mov nHigh, rax
        jmp .startSearch ; loop - try again with different high

.found:
        lea rdi, [searchStrFound]
        lea rsi, [pTemp]
        mov rdx, nIndex
        print
        jmp .fin

.notFound:
        lea rdi, [searchStrNotFound]
        lea rsi, [searchStr]
        print

.fin:
        epilogue

;==========================================================================
```

Activities

1. Create an assembly language program that performs a linear search on a sorted or unsorted array.
2. Modify bSearchString.asm to make it a recursive function (See Chapter 7).
3. Modify testStr.asm to perform five million searches of the array. Determine the times for a linear and a binary search. Do the results confirm your expectations?

CHAPTER 14

Finding, Reading, and Selecting File and Directory Metadata

The Linux ls utility program is a powerful tool that lists the contents of a Linux directory in alphanumeric order. Listing 14-1 shows a C implementation of the algorithm and Listing 14-2 shows an x64 assembly language implementation.

Listing 14-1. dir.c

```
///////////////////////////////////////////////////////////////////////////////
// dir.c
// John Schwartzman, Forte Systems, Inc.
// dir.c is a program to read the entries of a Linux file directory.
// 11/21/2023
///////////////////////////////////////////////////////////////////////////////

#include <stdio.h>
#include <string.h>
#include <stdlib.h>       // for EXIT_SUCCESS
#include <dirent.h>       // for dirent structure and file type information

int main(int argc, char *argv[])
{
    DIR*                  dir;
    struct dirent*        dirent;
    char*                 pFileType;
    int                   nEntries = 0;
```


J. Schwartzman, *Assembly Language Reimagined*, https://doi.org/10.1007/979-8-8688-1724-3_14

```
    if (argc == 1)
    {
        puts ("USAGE: dir dirname");
        return EXIT_FAILURE;
    }

    dir = opendir(argv[1]);

    if (dir != NULL)
    {
        while ((dirent = readdir(dir)) != NULL)
        {
            ++nEntries;
            switch (dirent->d_type)
            {
                case DT_REG:
                    pFileType = "reg";
                    break;

                case DT_DIR:
                    pFileType = "dir";
                    break;

                case DT_LNK:
                    pFileType = "link";
                    break;

                case DT_SOCK:
                    pFileType = "socket";
                    break;

                case DT_BLK:
                    pFileType = "block";

                case DT_CHR:
                    pFileType = "char";
                    break;

                default:
```

```
                pFileType = "unknown";
            }
            printf("\t%s (%s)\n", dirent->d_name, pFileType);
        }
        printf("%d entries were found.\n\n", nEntries);
    }
    closedir(dir);
    return EXIT_SUCCESS;
}
////////////////////////////////////////////////////////////////////////////
```

Listing 14-2. dir.asm

```
;==========================================================================
; dir.asm - retrieve directory info from the OS and print it
; John Schwartzman, Forte Systems, Inc.
; 11/25/2023
; Linux x86_64
;
;========================== CONSTANT DEFINITIONS ==========================
NUM_VAR             equu        6
ARG_SIZE            equ         8           ; size of argv vector
PATH_SEP            equ        47           ; ASCII '/' char
D_TYPE_OFFSET       equ        18           ; offset to dirent->d_type
D_NAME_OFFSET       equ        19           ; offset to dirent->d_name

%include "macro.inc"

global      main
extern      opendir, readdir, closedir      ; tell assembler/linker
about ext

DT_UNKNOWN          equ       0             ; dirent file types
DT_FIFO             equ       1
DT_CHR              equ       2
DT_BLK              equ       6
DT_DIR              equ       4
DT_REG              equ       8
```

```
DT_LNK              equ      10
DT_SOCK             equ      12

;======================== DEFINE LOCAL VARIABLES ========================
%define argc        qword [rsp + VAR_SIZE * (NUM_VAR - 6)]      ; rsp +  0
%define argv0       qword [rsp + VAR_SIZE * (NUM_VAR - 5)]      ; rsp +  8
%define dir         qword [rsp + VAR_SIZE * (NUM_VAR - 4)]      ; rsp + 16
%define type        qword [rsp + VAR_SIZE * (NUM_VAR - 3)]      ; rsp + 24
%define dirent      qword [rsp + VAR_SIZE * (NUM_VAR - 2)]      ; rsp + 32
%define nEntries    qword [rsp + VAR_SIZE * (NUM_VAR - 1)]      ; rsp + 40
;============================ CODE SECTION ==============================

section     .text

main:
      prologue NUM_VAR                      ; setup stack and space for 6
                                              local var
      mov      argc, rdi                    ; argc  = rdi (1st arg to main)
      mov      argv0, rsi                   ; argv0 = rsi (2nd arg to main)
      zero     rax
      mov      nEntries, rax

      cmp      rdi, 1                       ; more than 1 arg?
      je       .getDefaultPath              ;   jump if no

      lea      rdi, [path]                  ; rdi => path[]  <= dest
      mov      rsi, [rsi + ARG_SIZE]        ; rsi => argv[1] <= src
      strcpy
      jmp      .terminatePath

.getDefaultPath:
      strcpy      [path], [current_dir]    ;  path = "./"

.terminatePath:
      lea      rdi, [path]
      strlen                                ; rax = strlen(path)

      lea      rdi, [path]
      dec      rax                          ; rax => last char of path
```

```
        mov     dl, PATH_SEP
        cmp     [rdi + rax], dl             ; does rdi end with a '/'?
        je      .chdir                      ;       jump if yes

        inc     rax                         ; strlen++
        lea     rdi, [path]
        mov     [rdi + rax], dl             ; append '/'
        inc     rax                         ; strlen++
        zero    dl
        lea     rdi, [path]
        mov     [rdi + rax], dl             ; append EOL

.chdir:
        lea     rdi, [path]
        chdir                               ; getFileType needs us to chdir
        or      rax, rax                    ; successfully changed dir?
        je      .opendir                    ; jump if yes

        lea     rsi, [path]                 ; invalid directory selection
        print   [errFmt]                    ; print error message
        jmp     .fin                        ; and exit

.opendir:
        lea     rdi, [path]
        call    opendir                     ; rax = opendir(path)
        mov     dir, rax                    ; save dir
        rdflags rax                         ; is dir null?
        jz      .fin                        ; jump if yes

.top_of_loop:
        mov     rdi, dir
        call    readdir                     ; rax = readdir(dir)
        mov     dirent, rax                 ; dirent <= rax
        rdflags rax                         ; is dirent NULL?
        jz      .fin                        ; jump if yes (exit)

        rdstruc dirent, D_TYPE_OFFSET       ; get file  type
        mov     rax, [rdi]
```

```
        cmp     al, DT_REG
        lea     rdx, [dt_reg]               ; 3rd arg to print
        je      .printFileType

        cmp     al, DT_DIR
        lea     rdx, [dt_dir]               ; 3rd arg to print
        je      .printFileType

        cmp     al, DT_LNK
        lea     rdx, [dt_lnk]               ; 3rd arg to print
        je      .printFileType

        cmp     al, DT_FIFO
        lea     rdx, [dt_fifo]              ; 3rd arg to print
        je      .printFileType

        cmp     al, DT_CHR
        lea     rdx, [dt_chr]               ; 3rd arg to print
        je      .printFileType

        cmp     al, DT_BLK
        lea     rdx, [dt_blk]               ; 3rd arg to print
        je      .printFileType

        cmp     al, DT_SOCK
        lea     rdx, [dt_sock]              ; 3rd arg to print
        je      .printFileType

        lea     rdx, [dt_unknown]           ; 3rd arg to print

.printFileType:
        rdstruc dirent, D_NAME_OFFSET       ; get directory name
        lea     rsi, [rdi]                  ; 2nd arg to printf
        print   [prtFmt]                    ; 1st arg to printf
        inc     nEntries
        jmp     .top_of_loop                ; continue for other dir entries

.fin:
        mov     rsi, nEntries
```

```
    print     [prtFmtTotal]
    mov       rdi, dir
    call      closedir                  ; closedir(dir)
    epilogue

;======================== READ-ONLY DATA SECTION =======================
section      .rodata
prtFmt           db       TAB, "%s (%s)", LF, EOL
prtFmtTotal      db       "%2d entries found.", LF, LF, EOL
current_dir      db       "./", EOL
errFmt           db       "%s is not a valid directory!", LF, EOL
dt_unknown       db      "unknown", EOL            ; dirent file types
dt_fifo          db      "fifo", EOL
dt_chr           db      "char", EOL
dt_blk           db      "block", EOL
dt_dir           db      "dir", EOL
dt_reg           db      "reg", EOL
dt_lnk           db      "link", EOL
dt_sock          db      "socket", EOL

section  .bss
path      resb      256
;======================================================================
```

Activities

1. Modify dir.asm so that it does not list the . and .. directories. Call the new program dir2.asm and add it to Makefile.
2. Modify dir2.asm so that it only lists directories. Call the new program dir3.asm and add it to Makefile.
3. Modify dir3.asm so that it only lists non-directories. Call the new program dir4.asm.

4. Add command line switches to dir.asm so that it behaves like dir2.asm, dir3.asm, and dir4.asm. Call the new program dir5.asm and add it to Makefile.
5. Pipe dir through grep so that it only displays directories.
6. Pipe dir through grep so that it only displays regular files.

CHAPTER 15

Creating and Sorting a Linked List

We've seen in Chapters 12 and 13 that common information can be placed in an array of memory locations to be searched or sorted. In this chapter, we're going to place directory information, like that found by the ls utility, into a linked list. A linked list contains a memory allocation (malloc) for each node of information that we want to store. Each allocation also contains a pointer to the next piece of information. There is also a head node that points to the beginning of the list. Another type of linked list is bidirectional. It has next and prev members and can be navigated in either direction.

To search a linked list, we use the head node to navigate to the beginning of the list and then follow the next pointers until we find the entry we want. We'll know that we've reached the end of the list when we encounter a node where the next pointer points to head.

We'll add our quicksortStr and bubblesortStr assembly language implementations to our llDir executable so that we can sort the array of file objects.

Note that the implementation of our linked list is placed in its own module, listTools.asm (Listing 15-2). Also note the structure of our linked list node in the .bss uninitialized data section of listTools.asm. The STRUC macro also declares the equate, node_size, which states the size of our list nodes.

```
      STRUC    node         ; initialization of STRUCT node
nNameType      resb    ELEMENT_SIZE
nType          resb    16
nPrev          resq    1
nNext          resq    1
```


J. Schwartzman, *Assembly Language Reimagined*, https://doi.org/10.1007/979-8-8688-1724-3_15

```
        align   8     ; make sure we allocate on an 8-byte boundary
ENDSTRUC

ISTRUCT node          ; instantiation of STRUCT node
```

We'll use node_size to define our head node and all of the list node allocations in our program. We use the malloc macro to define all of this information. Look for the malloc node_size instruction in listTools.asm. Also, note the malloc macro in macro.inc.

In order to sort the linked list, we utilize a separate ordered integer listIndex to point to each node allocation. The listIndex array contains the starting address of each of our nodes.

A circular bidirectional linked list can be used to implement several important data structures: a stack (LIFO), a queue (FIFO), and a dqueue (a double ended queue).

The circular bidirectional linked list has an elegant feature: adding a new node to the list is always done in the same manner. We always add it to the front of the list, and there are no special cases.

To add a new node, we call malloc node_size, which returns a pointer to the new node in the rax register. Then we perform a little bit of housekeeping. We get the head node's next pointer and place it in the new node's prev pointer. After that, you make the head node's next pointer point to the new node and the new node's prev pointer point to the head node. The new node's next pointer is set to the value you got from the head node's next pointer.

In order to sort the linked list, we employ a different strategy. We create an array called listIndex which contains pointers to all of the nodes in our list.

The Makefile for llDir is shown in Listing 15-3. It assembles each .asm file separately into an object file. It then links llDir.obj to the other .obj files to form the executable file llDir. Please make sure that you understand every statement in Makefile.

The file llDir.asm is shown in Figure 15-1. Note that the implementation of our linked list is placed in its own module, listTools.asm (Listing 15-2).

Listing 15-1. `llDir.asm`

```
;==========================================================================
; llDir.asm - retrieve ls info from OS, sort & print it (ignores . and ..)
; John Schwartzman, Forte Systems, Inc.
; 12/03/2023
; Linux x86_64
;
```

```
;========================= CONSTANT DEFINITIONS =========================
NUM_VAR           equ        6         ; for main - round up to
even number
ARG_SIZE          equ        8         ; size of argv vector
PATH_SEP          equ       '/'        ; ASCII '/' char
D_NAME_OFFSET     equ       19         ; offset to dirent->d_name

%include "macro.inc"

%define __quicksort__


global     main
extern     opendir, readdir, closedir    ; extern procedures
extern     quicksortStr, bubblesortStr
extern     insertNode, traverseList
extern     freeList, createHeadNode

;===================== DEFINE LOCAL VARIABLES (main) ====================
%define argc      qword [rsp + VAR_SIZE * (NUM_VAR - 6)]      ; rsp +  0
%define argv0     qword [rsp + VAR_SIZE * (NUM_VAR - 5)]      ; rsp +  8
%define dir       qword [rsp + VAR_SIZE * (NUM_VAR - 4)]      ; rsp + 16
%define dirent    qword [rsp + VAR_SIZE * (NUM_VAR - 3)]      ; rsp + 24
%define nRec      qword [rsp + VAR_SIZE * (NUM_VAR - 2)]      ; rsp + 40

;============================= CODE SECTION =============================
section      .text

;========================================================================
main:
      prologue NUM_VAR                 ; setup stack and space for 6
local var
      mov      argc, rdi               ; argc  = rdi (1st arg to main)
      mov      argv0, rsi              ; argv0 = rsi (2nd arg to main)
      mov      nRec, 0                 ; zero record count

      cmp      rdi, 1                  ; more than 1 arg?
      je      .next0                   ; jump if no

      lea      rdi, [path]             ; rdi => path[]  <= dest
```

```
      mov      rsi, [rsi + ARG_SIZE]  ; rsi => argv[1] <= src
      strcpy
      jmp      .next1

.next0:
      lea      rdi, [path]
      lea      rsi, [cur_dir]                 ; src  => "./"
      mov      edx, MAX_PATH
      strncpy

.next1:
      lea      rdi, [path]
      strlen                                  ; rax = strlen(path)

      lea      rdi, [path]
      dec      rax                            ; rax => last char of path
      cmp      byte [rdi + rax], PATH_SEP     ; does rdi end with a '/'?
      je      .next2                          ; jump if yes

      inc      rax
      lea      rdi, [path]
      mov      byte [rdi + rax], PATH_SEP     ; append '/'
      inc      rax
      zero     dl
      lea      rdi, [path]
      mov      byte [rdi + rax], PATH_SEP     ; append EOL

.next2:
      chdir    [path]                         ; getFileType needs us
to chdir
      jz       .next3                         ; jump if chdir successfull

      lea      rsi, [path]                    ; invalid directory
selection
      print    [errFmt]                       ; print error message
      jmp      .err                           ; and exit

.next3:
      lea      rdi, [path]
```

```
    call     opendir                   ; rax = opendir(path)
    mov      dir, rax                  ; save dir
    rdflags  rax                       ; is dir null?
    jz       .err                      ; jump if yes

    call     createHeadNode

.top_of_loop:
    mov      rdi, dir
    call     readdir                   ; rax = readdir(dir)
    mov      dirent, rax               ; Dirent <- rax
    rdflags  rax                       ; is dirent NULL?
    jz       .fin                      ; jump if yes (exit)

        ; remove parent_dir (../) from list of files
        rdstruc dirent, D_NAME_OFFSET
        lea     rsi, [parent_dir]
        strcmp
        jz      .top_of_loop

        ; remove current_dir (./) from list of files
        rdstruc   dirent, D_NAME_OFFSET
        lea     rsi, [current_dir]
        strcmp
        jz      .top_of_loop

        ; save type and path of entry in new node
        rdstruc dirent, D_NAME_OFFSET
        lea      rsi, [rdi]
        lea      rdi, [dirNameT]
        strcpy

        rdstruc dirent, D_NAME_OFFSET
        call    getFileType            ; rax = getFileType
                                         (Dirent->d_name)
        strcat  [dirNameT], [rax]      ; concatenate filename and
                                         filetype

    ; create new node and insert it at the front of the list
```

```
        lea     rdi, [dirNameT]
        mov     rcx, nRec
        call    insertNode                  ; rdi -> noteName, rsi ->
                                              nodeType

        inc     nRec
        jmp     .top_of_loop                ; continue for other
                                              dir entries

.fin:
        puts    [unsorted]
        mov     rdi, nRec
        call    traverseList

%ifdef __bubblesort__

         puts   [bsorted]
        mov     rdi, 0                      ; i = nLow
        mov     rsi, nRec                   ; nHigh
        dec     rsi                         ; j = nHigh = nRec - 1
        call    bubblesortStr

%elifdef __quicksort__

        puts    [qsorted]
        mov     rdi, 0                      ; nLow = 0
        mov     rsi, nRec
        dec     rsi                         ; nHigh = number of
records - 1
        call    quicksortStr

%endif

        mov     rdi, nRec
        call    traverseList
        call    freeList

.err:
        mov     rdi, dir
```

```
    call     closedir                        ; closrdir(dir)
    puts     [blankline]
    epilogue EXIT_SUCCESS

;======================== READ-ONLY DATA SECTION ========================
section      .rodata
cur_dir      db "./", EOL
errFmt       db "ERROR: %s is not a valid directory!", LF, EOL
parent_dir   db  "..", EOL
current_dir  db  ".", EOL
blankline    db EOL
unsorted     db LF, "Insertion sorted List:", EOL
bsorted      db LF, "Bubblesorted List:", EOL
qsorted      db LF, "Quicksorted List:", EOL
spaceChar    db  " ", EOL
;======================= UNINITIALIZED DATA SECTION =====================
section .bss
path          resb      MAX_PATH
fileName      resb      64
fileType      resb      16
;========================================================================
```

Listing 15-2. listTools.asm

```
;========================================================================
; listTools.asm
; John Schwartzman, Forte Systems, Inc.
; 09/05/2024
; Linux x86_64
;
;========================================================================
ELEMENT_SIZE      equ            256

%include "macro.inc"

global      getElement, putElement, swap
extern      QuicksortStr, BubblesortStr           ; external procedures
extern      fileName, perm, sFileSize, sFileTime, sUid, sGid, nHardLinks
```

```
extern      begItemFmt
global      listIndex
global      array, pTemp, pTempi, pTempj      ; exported data
global      insertNode
global      traverseList, freeList
global      dspFmt, listIndex
global      n_sPerm, n_sSize, n_sTime, n_sNameLink
global      sFileInfo0, sFileInfo1, sFileInfo2, sFileInfo3

%define NODE_NAME                   0
%define NODE_PERM                  64
%define NODE_SIZE                  96
%define NODE_TIME                 112
%define NODE_NAME_LINK            128

%define     buffer      qword [rsp + 0]       ; for insertNode
%define     nRecords        qword [rsp + 0]      ; for traverseList

;=======================================================================
swap:
     prologue

     mov      rcx, r8
     lea      rdi, [pTempi]                    ; temp holding var
     call     getElement                       ; pTempi contains str from
                                                 array[i]

     mov      rcx, r9
     lea      rdi, [pTempj]                    ; temp holding var
     call     getElement                       ; pTempj contains str from
                                                 array[j]

     mov      rcx, r8
     lea      rsi, [nTempj]
     call     putElement                       ; rdi contains qword from
                                                 listIndex[]

     mov      rcx, r9
     lea      rsi, [nTempi]
```

```
        call    putElement                 ; rdi contains qword from
                                             listIndex[]

         epilogue

;==========================================================================
getElement:                           ; rcx = index, rsi = src,
rdi = dest
        mov     rsi, [listIndex + 8 * rcx]
        lea     rsi, [rsi + NODE_NAME]
        push    rcx
        strcpy
        pop     rcx
        ret                           ; rdi contains array[rcx]
on return

;==========================================================================
putElement:                           ; rcx = index, rsi = src,
rdi = dest
        mov     rsi, [listIndex + 8 * rcx]
        mov     rdi, [rsi]
        ret                           ; rdi contains listIndex + 8 * rcx
on return

;==========================================================================
freeList:
        mov     rax, [headNode]
        mov     rax, [rax + nNext]

.top:
        push    rax
        free    eax                   ; free the node
        pop     rax
        mov     rax, [rax + nNext]
        cmp     rax, [headNode]
        je      .fin
        jmp     .top
```

```
.fin:
      free      eax                         ; free headNode
      ret

;==============================================================================
createHeadNode:
      prologue

      malloc        ELEMENT_SIZE
      jz            .fin

      mov           [rax + nPrev], rax      ; head points back to itself
      mov           [rax + nNext], rax      ; head points forward to itself
      mov           [headNode], rax

.fin:
      epilogue

;==============================================================================
insertNode:                                 ; rcx contains number of records
      prologue 2

      test      rcx, rcx                    ; is numEntries 0
      jnz       .continue                   ;      jump if yes, createHeadNode
                                                   on nRecord 0

      call      createHeadNode
      zero      rcx

.continue:
      push      rcx
      malloc ELEMENT_SIZE                   ; dataNode_size = rax =>
allocation
      pop       rcx
      mov       [listIndex + 8 * rcx], rax        ; save allocation in
                                                    listIndex[]
      jz       .fin

      lea       rsi, [fileName]
      lea       rdi, [rax + NODE_NAME]
```

```
push      rcx                         ; save insertion index
push      rax
strcpy
pop       rax
pop       rcx

lea       rsi, [sFileInfo0]
lea       rdi, [rax + NODE_PERM]
push      rcx                         ; save insertion index
push      rax
strcpy
pop       rax
pop       rcx

push      rax                         ; get file size
lea       rsi, [sFileInfo1]
lea       rdi, [rax + NODE_SIZE]
strcpy                                ; copy file size into node
pop       rax

push      rax
lea       rsi, [sFileInfo2]
lea       rdi, [rax + NODE_TIME]
strcpy                                ; copy file mod time into node
pop       rax

push      rax
lea       rsi, [sFileInfo3]
lea       rdi, [rax + NODE_NAME_LINK]       ; copy sNameLink into node
strcpy
pop       rax

; housekeeping - insert new node at head->next
push       rcx

mov       rcx, [headNode]             ; get head node
mov       [rax + nPrev], rcx          ; new node prev = head

mov       rcx, [rcx + nNext]          ; rcx = head=>next
```

```
      mov       [rax + nNext], rcx          ; new node next = head->next

      mov       rcx, [headNode]
      mov       [rcx + nNext], rax          ; head->next = new node
                                            ; do not change head->prev
      pop       rcx

.fin:
      epilogue

;============================================================================
traverseList+                               ; retrieve the nodes the way
they're sorted
      prologue 2                            ; and not the way they're inserted
      mov       nRecords, rdi
      zero      rcx

.top:
      mov       rax, nRecords
      cmp       rcx, rax
      ; cmp     rcx, nRecords
      je       .fin

      push       rcx

      mov       r10, [listIndex + 8 * rcx]
      lea       rdi, [dspFmt]
      lea       rsi, [r10 + NODE_PERM]              ; perm, nHardLinks,
                                                      sUid, sPid
      lea       rdx, [r10 + NODE_SIZE]              ; file size
      lea       rcx, [r10 + NODE_TIME]              ; file time
      lea       r8,  [r10 + NODE_NAME_LINK]         ; file name, link
                                                      (if any), * if exe
      print                                         ; display contents of node

      pop       rcx
      inc       rcx
      jmp       .top
```

```
.fin:
      epilogue

;========================= READ-ONLY DATA SECTION =======================
section      .rodata
nameFmt      db  "%s", LF, EOL
prtInsTotal      db  TAB, LF, "%d elements were loaded.", LF, EOL
dspFmt      db  "%s%s%s%s", LF, EOL

;=========================================================================
section     .bss
pTemp       times 64      db 0
pTempi      times 64      db 0
pTempj      times 64      db 0
nTempi      resq             1
nTempj      resq             1

STRUC        dataNode                    ; declaration of dataNode
n_sName      resb        64
n_sPerm      resb        32
n_sSize      resb        16
n_sTime      resb        16
n_sNameLink  resb        64
nPrev        resq         1
nNext        resq         1
    ENDSTRUC

node       istruc      dataNode          ; assignment of dataNode
           iend

headNode    resq          1
listIndex   resq       1024              ; max number of linked list elements

sFileInfo0      resb      64
sFileInfo1      resb      16
sFileInfo2      resb      16
sFileInfo3      resb      64
;=========================================================================
```

Now build and execute llDir.

```
js@suse-tumbleweed-z4:~/Development/asm_x86_64/linkedList$ make .debug
yasm -f elf64 -g dwarf2 -D __quicksort__                    -o llDir.obj
llDir.asm
yasm -f elf64 -g dwarf2 -o quicksortStr.obj quicksortStr.asm
yasm -f elf64 -g dwarf2 -o bubblesortStr.obj bubblesortStr.asm
yasm -f elf64 -g dwarf2 -o listTools.obj listTools.asm
gcc -Wall -g -z noexecstack llDir.obj bubblesortStr.obj quicksortStr.obj
listTools.obj -o llDir
js@suse-tumbleweed-z4:~/Development/asm_x86_64/linkedList$ ./llDir
17 entries found.

Insertion sorted List:
        Makefile (reg)
        listTools.asm (reg)
        quicksortStr (reg)
        macro.inc (reg)
        quicksortStr.asm (reg)
        quicksortInt.asm (reg)
        bubblesortInt.asm (reg)
        bubblesortStr.asm (reg)
        llDir.asm (reg)
        quicksortStr.obj (reg)
        bubblesortStr.obj (reg)
        listTools.obj (reg)
        llDir.obj (reg)
        quicksortInt.obj (reg)
        bubblesortInt.obj (reg)
        debug (reg)
        llDir (reg)

Quicksorted List:
        bubblesortInt.asm (reg)
        bubblesortInt.obj (reg)
        bubblesortStr.asm (reg)
        bubblesortStr.obj (reg)
```

```
        debug (reg)
        listTools.asm (reg)
        listTools.obj (reg)
        llDir (reg)
        llDir.asm (reg)
        llDir.obj (reg)
        macro.inc (reg)
        Makefile (reg)
        quicksortInt.asm (reg)
        quicksortInt.obj (reg)
        quicksortStr (reg)
        quicksortStr.asm (reg)
        quicksortStr.obj (reg)
js@suse-tumbleweed-z4:~/Development/asm_x86_64/linkedList$
```

To see a greater variety of file types try $ `./llDir /dev`

Listing 15-3. The llDir Makefile

```
Quicksorted List:
        autofs (char)
        block (dir)
        bsg (dir)
        btrfs-control (char)
        bus (dir)
        cdrom (link)
        char (dir)
        console (char)
        core (link)
        cpu (dir)
        cpu_dma_latency (char)
        cuse (char)
        disk (dir)
        dmmidi (char)
        dri (dir)
        fb0 (char)
```

```
        fd (link)
        full (char)
        fuse (char)
        hidraw0 (char)
        hpet (char)
        hugepages (dir)
        hwrng (char)
        input (dir)
        kmsg (char)
        log (link)
        loop-control (char)
        loop0 (block)
        loop1 (block)
        …
```

```
###########################################################################
#
#       Makefile for llDir
#       John Schwartzman, Forte Systems, Inc.
#       12/03/2023
#
#       Commands:  make [.release], make .debug, make clean, make asm_c_prog
#                  make = make release
#       Requires:  ../maketest.sh
#
###########################################################################
INCLUDEFILE := macro.inc
SHELL       := /bin/bash
cc          := gcc
as          := yasm
ASM_FLAGS   := -f elf64
ASM_DFLAGS  := -f elf64 -g dwarf2
C_FLAGS     := -Wall -O3 -z noexecstack
C_DFLAGS    := -Wall -g -z noexecstack
DEPENDS     := $(wildcard *.asm) $(INCLUDEFILE) Makefile
DEF         := __quicksort__            # or __bubblesort__
```

```
.release: $(DEPENDS)
	@source ../maketest.sh && test .release .debug
	$(as) $(ASM_FLAGS) -D $(DEF) -o llDir.obj llDir.asm
	$(as) $(ASM_FLAGS) -o quicksortStr.obj quicksortStr.asm
	$(as) $(ASM_FLAGS) -o bubblesortStr.obj bubblesortStr.asm
	$(as) $(ASM_FLAGS) -o listTools.obj listTools.asm
	$(cc) $(C_FLAGS)      llDir.obj quicksortStr.obj bubblesortStr.obj \
	                      listTools.obj -o llDir

.debug: $(DEPENDS)
	@source ../maketest.sh && test .debug .release
	$(as) $(ASM_DFLAGS) -D $(DEF) -o llDir.obj llDir.asm
	$(as) $(ASM_DFLAGS) -o quicksortStr.obj quicksortStr.asm
	$(as) $(ASM_DFLAGS) -o bubblesortStr.obj bubblesortStr.asm
	$(as) $(ASM_DFLAGS) -o listTools.obj listTools.asm
	$(cc) $(C_DFLAGS) llDir.obj bubblesortStr.obj quicksortStr.obj
listTools.obj -o llDir

clean:
	rm -f *.obj .debug .release dir dir2 dir3 dir4 utility.*

###########################################################################
```

Activities

1. Modify the two sort routines so that they use strcasecmp (case insensitive string compare) rather than strcmp. This will result in a more recognizable alphabetization. For example, macro.inc should proceed Makefile rather than the other way around. Add macros to macro.inc for strcasecmp.

2. Add a symbolic link to point to llDir using the command shown here:

   ```
   $ ln -s llDir theExe
   ```

   Make sure that `$ ./theExe` executes `llDir`.

3. Modify your PATH environment variable to add $PWD to your path. Now try

```
$ theExe
```

   In order to permanently add $PWD to $PATH, you'll have to add the statement

```
export PATH=$PWD:$PATH
```

   to your ~/.bashrc properties file.

4. Implement sorting so that the directories are all shown before files. You could do this by adding a space in front of each node->n NameType. Why? When you want to print each directory name, start at position one instead of position zero. For example, print [strFormat], [strAddr + 1]. Modify traverseList to print the linked list Call your program llDir2.asm.

5. Add a command line flag (--dir_first) to your program so that users can specify on the command line whether they want to see directories before files in the sorted list.

```
$ llDir [--dis_first] [--dir_to_search = ./]
```

6. Modify llDir2.asm to use embedded ASCII escape characters to color code a sorted directory listing based on file type. Modify the traverseList method in order to color code your program's output.

7. Implement a stack using a circular doubly linked list. Implement push and pop methods.

8. Implement a queue using a circular doubly linked list. Implement push and pop methods.

9. Implement a dequeue using a circular doubly linked list. Implement push_front, pop_front, push_back and pop_back methods.

CHAPTER 16

Reading and Sorting File and Directory Information by Reading Directories

The Linux Shell (or List Status or List Summary) utility is a Linux shell command with many options. It is used to list *metadata* (information) about the files and directories present on disk. The ls command is often *aliased* to include some optional arguments. To use the *unaliased* version of ls, proceed "ls" at the Linux command prompt with the backslash character and you'll see something like this:

```
suse-tw-z4@~/Development/asm_x86_64/directory/ll$ \ls
bubblesortStr.asm  files          ll       macro.inc
runLL         theExe
fileInfo           fileSize.asm   ll.asm   Makefile         test.c
fileInfo.asm       fileTime.asm   lstat    maketest.sh      testDir.asm
fileInfo.c         listTools.asm  lstat.c  quicksortStr.asm test.s
```

The -lAFh options to ls provide a long, human-readable, file type classified display that displays hidden directories.

Each file or directory entry shows the file type, user, group and other file permissions, the number of hard links, the user name, the primary group name, the human-readable file size, the last modification time and date, and the file or directory name. The A option (almost all) indicates that hidden directories are shown, but not ./ and ../.

```
suse-tw-z4@~/Development/asm_x86_64/directory/ll$ \ls -lAFh
total 212K
-rw-r--r-- 1 js users 1.8K Aug 12 15:44 bubblesortStr.asm
-rw-r--r-- 1 js users    0 Aug 21 10:42 .debug
```


J. Schwartzman, *Assembly Language Reimagined*, https://doi.org/10.1007/979-8-8688-1724-3_16

```
-rwxr-xr-x 1 js users  24K Aug 18 15:11 fileInfo*
-rw-r--r-- 1 js users 8.8K Aug 21 10:41 fileInfo.asm
-rw-r--r-- 1 js users 4.3K Aug 18 15:11 fileInfo.c
drwxr-xr-x 2 js users 4.0K Aug  9 17:40 files/
-rw-r--r-- 1 js users 3.8K Aug 20 18:36 fileSize.asm
-rw-r--r-- 1 js users 1.7K Aug 21 10:30 fileTime.asm
drwxr-xr-x 8 js users 4.0K Aug 20 18:59 .git/
-rw-r--r-- 1 js users 5.5K Aug 11 15:02 listTools.asm
-rwxr-xr-x 1 js users  29K Aug 21 10:42 ll*
-rw-r--r-- 1 js users 4.6K Aug 20 18:15 ll.asm
-rwxr-xr-x 1 js users  24K Aug 18 06:36 lstat*
-rw-r--r-- 1 js users 2.5K Aug 17 16:53 lstat.c
-rw-r--r-- 1 js users 7.1K Aug 14 16:14 macro.inc
-rw-r--r-- 1 js users 2.0K Aug 12 18:02 Makefile
-rw-r--r-- 1 js users  707 Jul 23 15:14 maketest.sh
-rw-r--r-- 1 js users 2.2K Aug 12 15:43 quicksortStr.asm
-rwxr-xr-x 1 js users  29K Aug  9 17:18 runLL*
-rw-r--r-- 1 js users  408 Aug 17 16:42 test.c
-rw-r--r-- 1 js users 4.6K Jul 23 15:19 testDir.asm
-rw-r--r-- 1 js users 1.3K Aug  8 19:03 test.s
lrwxrwxrwx 1 js users    2 Jul 26 14:58 theExe -> ll*
drwxr-xr-x 2 js users 4.0K Aug 18 15:10 .vscode/
```

For example, the entry for ll shows that ll is a regular executable file. Its owner is js and the primary group is users. The owner, js, has read, write, and execute permissions to the file and the primary group, users, has read and execute permissions to ll. All other users have read and execute permissions only. The ll file has one hard link (the file itself). The ll file is 29KB in size, and it was last modified on August 21 at 10:42 pm. The final character, "*", indicates that ll is executable.

We're now going to write the ll (ls -lAFh) utility program in assembly language. The file ll.asm starts the action by iterating through the files and directories contained in the current directory. The file fileInfo.asm handles the file type and permissions, the number of hard links, and an entry's user and group. The file fileSize.asm handles the human readable file size property, and fileTime.asm handles the time and date of the last file modification. Both readFileSize and readFileTime are called by fileInfo.asm.

The linked list of files and directories is indexed and sorted by file name. The file quicksortStr.asm or bubblesortStr.asm takes care of sorting the linked list. We use the same versions of these two files that we used in Chapter 15 (llDir).

The function readFileSize determines whether it needs to perform a division operation at all, and otherwise, whether it must perform an integer or a floating point division. To determine whether an integer division is all that's needed, we perform a modulus operation. That's an integer division: the remainder is the modulus of the operatives. A modulus of zero means no remainder; therefore, an integer division will suffice.

Alas, things are not always what they seem. The description of the stat C structure is provided by the internet as

```
struct stat
{
    dev_t     st_dev;     /* ID of device containing file */
    ino_t     st_ino;     /* inode number */
    mode_t    st_mode;    /* protection */
    nlink_t   st_nlink;   /* number of hard links */
    uid_t     st_uid;     /* user ID of owner */
    gid_t     st_gid;     /* group ID of owner */
    dev_t     st_rdev;    /* device ID (if special file) */
    off_t     st_size;    /* total size, in bytes */
    blksize_t st_blksize; /* blocksize for file system I/O */
    blkcnt_t  st_blocks;  /* number of 512B blocks allocated */
    time_t    st_atime;   /* time of last access */
    time_t    st_mtime;   /* time of last modification */
    time_t    st_ctime;   /* time of last status change */
};
```

When I tried to use this structure, I found that the order and size of the structure elements were not as described by the internet. The small C program, fileInfo.c, shows the actual sizes and order of the structure elements.

```
suse-tw-z4@~/Development/asm_x86_64/directory/ll$ ./fileInfo
File path: fileInfo.c
uid: 1000, gid: 100
mode: 100644 (octal)
```

```
uid: js, gid: users
File: fileInfo.c
hard links: 1
Permissions: -rw-r--r--
File size: 4342
mTime =  Aug 20 15:21

st_dev:      0           // stat structure
st_ino:      8
st_mode:     24          // NOTE: This element is out of order.
st_nlink:    16
st_uid:      28
st_gid:      32
st_rdev:     40
st_size:     48
st_blksize: 56
st_blocks:   64
st_atime:    72
st_mtime:    88          // NOTE: This element is too large.
st_ctime:    104

pw_name:     0
pw_passwd:   8
pw_uid:      16
pw_gid:      20
pw_gecos:    24
pw_dir:      32
pw_shell     40

gw_name:     0
gw_passwd:   8
gw_gid:      16
gw_mem:      24
```

This shows that certain elements of stat have different order and sizes from the structure shown in the documentation. The solution is to construct the structure in our assembly language program as it appears from compiling and executing fileInfo.c. This is what we have done in fileInfo.asm.

Compile fileInfo.c using **gcc -Wall -g fileInfo.c -o fileInfo** and then execute fileInfo. In fileInfo.asm, define stat64 and its offsets as shown in the output of fileInfo.

Listing 16-1. The fileInfo.c Utility Program

```
//==========================================================================
// fileInfo.c
// John Schwartzman, Forte Systems, Inc.
// 08/18/2024
// Linux x86_64
//==========================================================================

#include <stdio.h>
#include <stdlib.h>
#include <sys/stat.h>
#include <sys/types.h>
#include <pwd.h>
#include <grp.h>
#include <stddef.h>
#include <time.h>

struct stat          st;
struct passwd*       pw;
struct group*        gr;

const char*          pFilePath = "fileInfo.c";
char                 filePerm[] = { '-', '-', '-', '-', '-', '-', '-', '-',
                                    '-', '-', 0};

// printFileAppDateTime
int printFileAppDateTime(long mTime)
{
      char             pDateTime[28];
      struct tm*       tmp;
      int              nRetVal;

      tmp = localtime(&mTime);
      nRetVal = strftime(pDateTime, 28,  " %b %d %H:%M\n", tmp);
      if(nRetVal == 0)
```

```
    {
        return EXIT_FAILURE;      // not enough space for pDateTime
    }

    printf("mTime = %s\n", pDateTime);
    return EXIT_SUCCESS;
}

// printFileInfo
int printFileInfo()
{
    // perform lstat on pFilePath and place result in st
    int      nResult = lstat(pFilePath, &st);

    if (nResult != 0)
        {
            return nResult;
        }

    printf("File path: %s\n", pFilePath);
    printf("uid: %d, gid: %d\n", st.st_uid, st.st_gid);

    printf("mode: %o (octal)\n", st.st_mode);

    // invoke getpwuid
    pw = getpwuid(st.st_uid);

    // invoke getgrgid
    gr = getgrgid(st.st_gid);

    printf("uid: %s, gid: %s\n", pw->pw_name, gr->gr_name);

    unsigned int nType = (st.st_mode) & __S_IFMT;

    if (nType == __S_IFREG)
        filePerm[0] = '-';
    else if (nType == __S_IFDIR)
        filePerm[0] = 'd';
    else if (nType == __S_IFLNK)
```

```
        filePerm[0] = 'l';
else if (nType == __S_IFIFO)
        filePerm[0] = 'p';
else if (nType == __S_IFSOCK)
        filePerm[0] = 's';
else if (nType == __S_IFBLK)
        filePerm[0] = 'b';
else if (nType == __S_IFCHR)
        filePerm[0] = 'c';

if (st.st_mode & S_IRUSR)
        filePerm[1] = 'r';
else
        filePerm[1] = '-';

if (st.st_mode & S_IWUSR)
        filePerm[2] = 'w';
else
        filePerm[2] = '-';

if (st.st_mode & S_IXUSR)
        filePerm[3] = 'x';
else
        filePerm[3] = '-';

if (st.st_mode & S_IRGRP)
        filePerm[4] = 'r';
else
        filePerm[4] = '-';

if (st.st_mode & S_IWGRP)
        filePerm[5] = 'w';
else
        filePerm[5] = '-';

if (st.st_mode & S_IXGRP)
        filePerm[6] = 'x';
else
```

```
        filePerm[6] = '-';

    if (st.st_mode & S_IROTH)
        filePerm[7] = 'r';
    else
        filePerm[7] = '-';

    if (st.st_mode & S_IWOTH)
        filePerm[8] = 'w';
    else
        filePerm[8] = '-';

    if (st.st_mode & S_IXOTH)
        filePerm[9] = 'x';
    else
        filePerm[9] = '-';

    // print info collected by printFileInfo
    printf("File: %s\n", pFilePath);
    printf("hard links: %ld\n", st.st_nlink);
    printf("Permissions: %s\n", filePerm);
    printf("File size: %ld\n", st.st_size);
    printFileAppDateTime(st.st_atime);

    printf("st_dev:     %ld\n", offsetof(struct stat, st_dev));
    printf("st_ino:     %ld\n", offsetof(struct stat, st_ino));
    printf("st_mode:    %ld\n", offsetof(struct stat, st_mode));
    printf("st_nlink:   %ld\n", offsetof(struct stat, st_nlink));
    printf("st_uid:     %ld\n", offsetof(struct stat, st_uid));
    printf("st_gid:     %ld\n", offsetof(struct stat, st_gid));
    printf("st_rdev:    %ld\n", offsetof(struct stat, st_rdev));
    printf("st_size:    %ld\n", offsetof(struct stat, st_size));
    printf("st_blksize: %ld\n", offsetof(struct stat, st_blksize));
    printf("st_blocks:  %ld\n", offsetof(struct stat, st_blocks));
    printf("st_atime:   %ld\n", offsetof(struct stat, st_atime));
    printf("st_mtime:   %ld\n", offsetof(struct stat, st_mtime));
    printf("st_ctime:   %ld\n", offsetof(struct stat, st_ctime));
    printf("\n");
```

```
printf("pw_name:    %ld\n", offsetof(struct passwd, pw_name));
printf("pw_passwd:  %ld\n", offsetof(struct passwd, pw_passwd));
printf("pw_uid:     %ld\n", offsetof(struct passwd, pw_uid));
printf("pw_gid:     %ld\n", offsetof(struct passwd, pw_gid));
printf("pw_gecos:   %ld\n", offsetof(struct passwd, pw_gecos));
printf("pw_dir:     %ld\n", offsetof(struct passwd, pw_dir));
printf("pw_shell    %ld\n", offsetof(struct passwd, pw_shell));
printf("\n");

printf("gw_name:    %ld\n", offsetof(struct group, gr_name));
printf("gw_passwd:  %ld\n", offsetof(struct group, gr_passwd));
printf("gr_gid:     %ld\n", offsetof(struct group, gr_gid));
printf("gr_mem:     %ld\n", offsetof(struct group, gr_mem));
```

The file fileInfo.asm is used to return the *metadata* of the variable fileName. It places this information into a human-readable string. The %define definitions were found in the glibc header file stat.h. Note that fileInfo.asm begins by finding the file type, followed by the user permissions. It also finds the user's UID and GID in string format.

The key to decoding the file type and file permissions is to retrieve the st_mode word from the stat64 structure and to AND it with the octal value S_IFMT. We use the result of this AND to obtain the file type byte and the nine permission bytes – for owner, owner's group, and other users – and we put these bytes into the perm string variable.

We then call the assembly language modules readFileSize and readFileTime.

Listing 16-2. fileInfo.asm

```
;==============================================================================
; fileInfo.asm
; John Schwartzman, Forte Systems, Inc.
; 08/20/2024
; Linux x86_64
;==============================================================================
%include "macro.inc"

global readFileInfo
extern readFileSize
extern readFileTime
global begItemFmt
```

```
global perm, sUid, sGid, nHardLinks
global mtime, msize, fileName
extern sFileInfo0, sFileInfo1, sFileInfo2, sFileInfo3
extern listIndex, n_sPerm, n_sSize, n_sTime, n_sNameLink
global totalBytes

%define S_IFMT 0170000q ; q is necessary to indicate octal values

%define S_IFSOCK 0140000q ; socket - from <sys/stat.h>
%define S_IFLNK 0120000q ; hard link
%define S_IFREG 0100000q ; regular file
%define S_IFBLK 0060000q ; block device
%define S_IFDIR 0040000q ; directory
%define S_IFCHR 0020000q ; character device
%define S_IFIFO 0010000q ; fifo (pipe)

%define S_IRUSR 0400q ; Read by owner
%define S_IWUSR 0200q ; Write by owner
%define S_IXUSR 0100q ; Execute by owner
%define S_IRGRP 0040q ; Read by group
%define S_IWGRP 0020q ; Write by group
%define S_IXGRP 0010q ; Execute by group
%define S_IROTH 0004q ; Read by others
%define S_IWOTH 0002q ; Write by others
%define S_IXOTH 0001q ; Execute by others

%define st_dev 0 ; struct stat64
%define st_ino 8
%define st_nlink 16
%define st_mode 24
%define st_uid 28
%define st_gid 32
%define st_rdev 40
%define st_size 48
%define st_blksize 56
%define st_blocks 64
%define st_atime 72
```

```
%define st_mtime 88
%define st_ctime 104

%define pw_name 0 ; struct pw
%define pw_passwd 8
%define pw_uid 16
%define pw_gid 20
%define pw_gecos 24
%define pw_dir 32
%define pw_shell 40

%define gr_name 0 ; struct gw
%define gr_passwd 8
%define gr_gid 16
%define gr_mem 24

%define NUM_VAR 2 ; round up to next even value

;=============== DEFINE LOCAL VARIABLES for readFileInfo =================
%define buffer qword [rsp + VAR_SIZE * (NUM_VAR - 2)] ; rsp + 0

;============================= CODE SECTION ================================
section .text

;=========================================================================
readFileInfo:
prologue NUM_VAR ; leave room for stack variable buffer

mov rdi, rsi
lea rsi, [stat64]
lstat ; fill stat64 structure for this file
cmp rax, -1
je .err1 ; error - return with rax = -1

lea eax, dword [stat64 + st_uid]
mov esi, dword [eax]

lea rsi, qword [stat64 + st_mode] ; get mode
mov esi, [rsi]
```

```
mov [nMode], esi

lea rdi, [stat64 + st_uid] ; get uid
mov rdi, [rdi]
getpwuid ; get struc password
mov [pw], rax

lea rdi, [pw] ; get gid name
mov rax, [rdi] ; save struc password

lea rdi, [stat64 + st_gid] ; get gid
mov rdi, [rdi]
getgrgid ; get struc group
mov [gw], rax ; save struc group
lea rdi, [sUid] ; copy uid name
mov rsi, [pw]
mov rsi, [rsi]
strcpy

lea rdi, [sGid] ; copy gid name
mov rsi, [gw]
mov rsi, [rsi]
strcpy

lea rdi, [stat64 + st_nlink] ; get hard links
mov rdi, [rdi]
mov [nHardLinks], rdi

lea rdi, [stat64 + st_size] ; get file size
mov rdi, [rdi]
mov [nFileSize], rdi

lea rdi, [stat64 + st_mtime] ; get file modification time
mov rdi, [rdi]
mov [nFileTime], rdi

lea rsi, [roperm] ; init permissions
lea rdi, [perm]
strcpy
```

```
mov eax, [nMode]
and eax, S_IFMT ; check file type

cmp rax, S_IFREG ; regular file
je .gotFileType

cmp rax, S_IFDIR ; directory
mov byte [perm], 'd'
je .gotFileType

cmp rax, S_IFLNK ; link
mov byte [perm], 'l'
je .gotFileType

cmp rax, S_IFIFO ; pipe (FIFO)
mov byte [perm], 'p'
je .gotFileType

cmp rax, S_IFSOCK ; socket
mov byte [perm], 's'
je .gotFileType

cmp rax, S_IFBLK ; block device
mov byte [perm], 'b'
je .gotFileType

cmp rax, S_IFCHR ; character device
mov byte [perm], 'c'
je .gotFileType

mov byte [perm], '?'

.gotFileType: ; now check file permissions
mov eax, [nMode]
test eax, S_IRUSR ; owner read
jz .gotUserRead
mov byte [perm + 1], 'r'

.gotUserRead:
test eax, S_IWUSR ; owner write
```

```
jz .gotUserWrite
mov byte [perm + 2], 'w'

.gotUserWrite:
test eax, S_IXUSR ; owner execute
jz .gotUserExecute
mov byte [perm + 3], 'x'

.gotUserExecute:
test eax, S_IRGRP ; group read
jz .gotGroupRead
mov byte [perm + 4], 'r'

.gotGroupRead:
test eax, S_IWGRP ; group write
jz .gotGroupWrite
mov byte [perm + 5], 'w'

.gotGroupWrite:
test eax, S_IXGRP ; group execute
jz .gotGroupExecute
mov byte [perm + 6], 'x'

.gotGroupExecute:
test eax, S_IROTH ; other read
jz .gotOtherRead
mov byte [perm + 7], 'r'

.gotOtherRead:
test eax, S_IWOTH ; other write
jz .gotOtherWrite
mov byte [perm + 8], 'w'

.gotOtherWrite:
test eax, S_IXOTH ; other execute
jz .printPermissions
mov byte [perm + 9], 'x'
```

```
.printPermissions:
cmp byte [perm], 'l' ; is the current file a link?
jne .next ; jump if no

readlink [fileName], [linkName], 64 ; read linkName
cmp rax, -1
je .err2

.next:
lea rdi, [sFileInfo0] ; load file type, perm, uid, gid
lea rsi, [begItemFmt]
lea rdx, [perm]
mov rcx, [nHardLinks]
lea r8, [sUid]
lea r9, [sGid]
sprint
mov rdi, [nFileSize] ; get file size
add [totalBytes], rdi ; accumulate file sizes
call readFileSize ; create human interface

lea rsi, [rax] ; get returned buffer into rsi
lea rdi, [sFileInfo1]
sprint ; copy file size string into sFileInfo1

lea rdi, [nFileTime] ; get file mod time
call readFileTime ; create string version

lea rsi, [rax] ; calculate ds
lea rdi, [sFileInfo2]
strcpy

cmp byte [perm], 'l' ; is the node a link?
je .next2 ; jump if yes

lea rsi, [fileName]
lea rdi, [sFileInfo3]
strcpy ; buffer now contains fileName only
jmp .fin
```

```
.next2:
lea rdi, [sFileInfo3] ; output buffer
lea rsi, [linkNameFmt]
lea rdx, [fileName]
lea rcx, [linkName]
sprint
jmp .fin

cmp byte [perm + 9], 'x' ; is the link executable by everyone
jne .fin ; jump if no

strcat [sNameLink], [pAsterisk] ; the link is executable
strcpy [sFileInfo3], [sNameLink]
jmp .fin

.err1:
perror [lstatName] ; return errno
jmp .exit

.err2:
perror [rdlinkName] ; return errno
jmp .exit

.fin:
cmp byte [perm], 'd' ; is the node a directory?
je .fin2 ; jump if yes (don't append '*')

cmp byte [perm + 9], 'x' ; is the node executable by everyone?
jne .fin2 ; jump if no

strcat [sFileInfo3], [pAsterisk] ; sNameLink is executable

.fin2:
zero eax ; return EXIT_SUCCESS

.exit:
epilogue
;==========================================================================
section .bss
```

```
struc stat64_struct ; structure declaration
ST_DEV resq 1 ; stat_struct + 0
ST_INO resq 1 ; + 8
ST_MODE resd 1 ; + 16 file type and permissions
ST_NLINK resq 1 ; + 20 NOTE: ORDER OF TERMS
ST_UID resd 1 ; + 28
ST_GID resd 1 ; + 32
ST_FILL1 resd 1 ; + 36 NOTE: ADDITION OF FILL TERM
ST_RDEV resq 1 ; + 40
ST_SIZE resq 1 ; + 48
ST_BLKSIZE resq 1 ; + 56
ST_BLOCKS resq 1 ; + 64
ST_ATIME resq 1 ; + 72
ST_MTIME resq 1 ; + 88 NOTE: ORDER OF TERMS
ST_CTIME resq 1 ; + 104
endstruc

struc pw_struct ; structure declaration
PW_NAME resq 1
PW_PASSWD resq 1
PW_UID resd 1
PW_GID resd 1
PW_GECOS resq 1
PW_DIR resq 1
PW_SHELL resq 1
endstruc

struc gr_struct ; structure declaration
GR_NAME resq 1
GR_SIZE resq 1
GR_PASSWD resq 1
GR_GID resd 1
endstruc

sUid resb 16
sGid resb 16
nFileSize resq 1
```

```
nFileTime resq 1
nMode resd 1
linkName resb 64
fileName resb 64
sNameLink resb 64

section .data

nHardLinks dq 0
perm db '-', '-', '-', '-', '-', '-', '-', '-', '-', '-', ' ', EOL
totalBytes dq 0

stat64 istruc stat64_struct
iend

pw istruc pw_struct
iend

gw istruc gr_struct
iend

section .rodata

lstatName db "lstat returned", EOL
rdlinkName db "rdlink returned", EOL
linkNameFmt db "%s -> %s", EOL
pAsterisk db "*", EOL
pFmt db "%s", EOL
begItemFmt db "%s%lld %s %s ", EOL ; perm, nHardLinks, sUid, sGid
roperm db '-', '-', '-', '-', '-', '-', '-', '-', '-', '-', ' ', EOL

;==============================================================================
```

The function readFileSize (fileSize.asm) is invoked to convert the file size into a human-readable string in engineering format. Note that as we continuously reduce the dividend, we continuously increase the exponent. For example, a file size of 1000 returns the string 1K and a file size of 1000000 returns the string 1M.

Our file sizes are smaller than those produced by ls -lAFh, because we're simply finding the file size while ls is finding the space consumed on disk by a file.

Listing 16-3. fileSize.asm

```
;==========================================================================
; fileSize.asm
; John Schwartzman, Forte Systems, Inc.
; 08/20/2024
; Linux x86_64
;==========================================================================
%include      "macro.inc"

global       readFileSize, printFileSize
extern       fileName

%define DIVISOR       1000
%define PETABYTE      DIVISOR * DIVISOR * DIVISOR * DIVISOR * DIVISOR
%define TERABYTE      DIVISOR * DIVISOR * DIVISOR * DIVISOR
%define GIGABYTE      DIVISOR * DIVISOR * DIVISOR
%define MEGABYTE      DIVISOR * DIVISOR
%define KILOBYTE      DIVISOR

%define      NUM_VAR      4             ; round up to next even value

;================ DEFINE LOCAL VARIABLES for readFileSize ================
%define   nSize      qword [rsp + VAR_SIZE * (NUM_VAR - 4)]      ; rsp +  0
%define   nDividend  qword [rsp + VAR_SIZE * (NUM_VAR - 3)]      ; rsp +  8
%define   buffer     qword [rsp + VAR_SIZE * (NUM_VAR - 2)]      ;
rsp +  16

;============================ CODE SECTION ===============================
section      .text

printFileSize:                              ; rdi contains file size
      prologue

      call       readFileSize           ; formatted output string is
left in rax
      lea      rdi, [rax]                   ; get return value from readFileSize
      print

      epilogue
```

```
;==========================================================================
readFileSize:
      prologue NUM_VAR

      mov       nSize, rdi
      mov       rax, nSize
      cmp       rax, DIVISOR
      jb       .belowDivisor               ; jump if nSize < 1000

      mov       rax, [sizeArray]
      mov       nDividend, rax
      xor       rcx, rcx                   ; loop count - initialization
                                             for loop

.topOfLoop:
      mov       nDividend, rax             ; if (nSize < nDividend) continue
      cmp       nSize, rax
      jb       .bottomOfLoop
      jmp       .proceed

.bottomOfLoop:
      inc       rcx                        ; increment loop count
      mov       rax, [sizeArray + 8 * rcx]
      mov       nDividend, rax
      jmp       .topOfLoop

.proceed:
      mod       nSize, nDividend           ; is there a remainder?
      jz       .integerDivide              ; no remainder
      jmp       .nonIntegerDivide

.integerDivide:                            ; perform integer division
      mov       rax, nSize                 ; divide nSize / nMultiplicand
      mov       r8, nDividend
      cdqe                                 ; sign extend rax into rdx
      div       r8
      lea       rdi, buffer
      lea       rsi, [szModMultiplierZero]  ; prepare to print result
```

```
      mov      rdx, rax                    ;  rax contains the quotient
      mov      cl,      byte [rangeArray + rcx]
      sprint
      jmp      .fin

.nonIntegerDivide:                         ; perform the floating point
                                             division

      movsd    xmm0, nSize
      movsd    xmm1, nDividend
      divsd    xmm0, xmm1
      lea      rdi, buffer
      lea      rsi, [szModMultiplierNotZero]
      zero     rdx
      mov      dl, byte [rangeArray + rcx]
      mov      eax, ONE
      call     sprintf
      jmp      .fin

.belowDivisor:
      lea      rdi, buffer
      lea      rsi, [szFmt]
      mov      rdx, nSize
      sprint

.fin:
      lea      rax, buffer

.exit:
      epilogue

;==========================================================================

%ifdef __
MAIN__      ;===========================================================

main:
      prologue

       mov      rcx, -1                               ; starting position
```

```
.runFileSize:
      inc      rcx
      push     rcx
      mov      rdi, [nFileSizes + 8 * rcx]
      cmp      rdi, ZERO             ; sentinal value
      jl      .fin

      call     printFileSize
      putchar  LF
      pop      rcx
      jmp      .runFileSize

.fin:
      epilogue

%endif  ;==================== __MAIN__ ====================================


;=============================================================================
section            .rodata

szFmt                          db      "%5lld ", EOL
szModMultiplierZero            db      "%4lld.0%c ", EOL
szModMultiplierNotZero         db      "%4.1f%c ", EOL

rangeArray                     db      'P', 'T', 'G', 'M', 'K'

sizeArray                      dq            PETABYTE, \
                                             TERABYTE, \
                                             GIGABYTE, \
                                             MEGABYTE, \
                                                KILOBYTE

section     .data

nFileSize                      dq      0

%ifdef __MAIN__;=============================================================

nFileSizes  dq           0,           0,                10,          100, 999,
```

```
        dq          1000,         1121,             21000,      22007,
        dq          22107,        1250000,          135000000,
        dq          13500000000, 13500000000000, 0,              -1

%endif;==================== __MAIN__ ====================================
;=========================================================================
```

Listing 16-4. fileTime.asm

```
    ;=====================================================================

    The function fileTime is also invoked by fileInfo.asm to return the
last modification time of the file in time and date format. The formatted
file time string is returned in buffer. FileTime.asm calls the glibc
functions localtime and strftime to turn the file modification time into
a string.

;=========================================================================
; fileTime.asm
; John Schwartzman, Forte Systems, Inc.
; 08/20/2024
; Linux x86_64
;=========================================================================
%include "macro.inc"

global readFileTime

%define NUM_VAR 2 ; round up to next even value

;================= DEFINE LOCAL VARIABLES for readFileTime ===============
%define buffer qword [rsp + VAR_SIZE * (NUM_VAR - 2)] ; rsp + 0

;============================ CODE SECTION ================================
section .text

;==========================================================================
=
readFileTime:
prologue NUM_VAR

localtime               ; edi contains the file modification time
```

```
mov [tm], rax

lea rdi, buffer
mov rsi, 40 ; size of buffer
lea rdx, [tdFmt]
mov rcx, [tm]
strftime
lea rax, buffer ; return buffer to caller in rax

epilogue

;===========================================================================
section .rodata

tdFmt db "%b %-2d %H:%M ", EOL

section .bss

struc tm_type              ; structure declaration
      tm_sec resd   1
      tm_min resd   1
      tm_hour resd  1
      tm_mday resd  1
      tm_mon resd   1
      tm_year resd  1
      tm_wday resd  1
      tm_yday resd  1
      tm_isdst resd 1
endstruc

tm istruc tm_type              ; structure implementation
iend

;===========================================================================
```

Listing 16-5. myll.asm

```
      ;=======================================================================
```

The file myll.asm uses opendir, readdir and closedir to access the files in a directory and invokes readFileInfo, which, in turn, invokes readFileSize and readFileTime. This turns the file metadata into a human readable string which is placed into our linked list or retrieval using the function traverseList. The linked list is alphabetized by myll.asm before retrieval.

```
;===============================================================================
; myll.asm - retrieve ls info from the OS, sort & print it as ls -lAFh
; John Schwartzman, Forte Systems, Inc.
; Fri Oct 11 05:28:19 PM EDT 2024
; Linux x86_64
;
;========================= CONSTANT DEFINITIONS ========================
NUM_VAR equ 6 ; for main - round up to even number
D_NAME_OFFSET equ 19 ; offset to dirent->d_name

%include "macro.inc"

global main
extern fileName
extern readFileInfo, readFileSize, printFileSize
extern quicksortStr
extern insertNode, traverseList, freeList
extern listIndex
extern totalBytes

;===================== DEFINE LOCAL VARIABLES (main) ====================
%define argc qword [rsp + VAR_SIZE * (NUM_VAR - 6)] ; rsp + 0
%define argv0 qword [rsp + VAR_SIZE * (NUM_VAR - 5)] ; rsp + 8
%define dir qword [rsp + VAR_SIZE * (NUM_VAR - 4)] ; rsp + 16
%define dirent qword [rsp + VAR_SIZE * (NUM_VAR - 3)] ; rsp + 24
%define nRecords qword [rsp + VAR_SIZE * (NUM_VAR - 2)] ; rsp + 40

;============================= CODE SECTION ==============================
section .text

;===============================================================================
```

```
main:
prologue NUM_VAR ; setup stack for 6 local var (5 + 1)
mov argc, rdi ; argc = rdi (1st arg to main)
mov argv0, rsi ; argv0 = rsi (2nd arg to main)
zero rax
mov nRecords, rax ; zero record count

getcwd [path], 256 ; set path to current working directory

mov rdi, argc
cmp rdi, ONE ; only one cmd line argument (myll itself)?
je .opendir ; jump if yes

print [usageErr] ; we shouldn't get here if myll called with 1 arg
jmp .exit

lea rdi, [path] ; append '/' to path
lea rsi, [path_sep]
strcat

lea rdi, [path] ; append argv[1] to path
mov rsi, argv0
mov rsi, [rsi + ARG_SIZE]
strcat

lea rdi, [path] ; append '/' to path
lea rsi, [path_sep]
strcat

; try iterating over argv[] here
mov r9, 0
mov rax, argc

mov r8, argv0
cmp r8, rax
jz .fin
mov rsi, [rax + r9 * ARG_SIZE] ; current file name
lea rdi, [fileName]
strcpy
```

```
jmp .insert

inc r9
cmp r9, argc
jne .exit

.chdir:
chdir [path] ; getFileType needs us to chdir
jz .opendir ; jump if chdir successfull

lea rsi, [path] ; invalid directory selection
print [errFmt] ; print error message
jmp .exit ; and exit

.opendir:
lea rdi, [path]
opendir ; rax = opendir(path)
mov dir, rax ; save dir
jz .exit ; jump if dir = null

.top_of_loop:
mov rdi, dir
readdir ; rax = readdir(dir)
mov dirent, rax ; Dirent <- rax
jz .fin ; jump to .fin if dirent = null

rdstruc dirent, D_NAME_OFFSET ; get directory name
lea rsi, [rdi]
lea rdi, [fileName]
strcpy ; copy fileName

; parent directory filter
lea rsi, [parent_dir] ; skip parent dir
strcmp
jz .top_of_loop

; current directory filter
lea rsi, [this_dir] ; skip currrent dir
strcmp
```

```
jz .top_of_loop

; If cmdline includes a wildcard, all files matching the wildcard
; are included on the command line.

.insert: ; create new node and insert it at the front of the list
lea rsi, [fileName]
mov rcx, nRecords
call readFileInfo ; get file metadata including size and time
mov rcx, nRecords
call insertNode ; create new element - rsi => array[rcx]
inc nRecords ; point to next record
jmp .top_of_loop ; continue for other dir entries

.fin: ; reached end of directory
zero rdi ; nLow = 0
mov rsi, nRecords
dec rsi ; nHigh = number of records - 1
call quicksortStr

print [totalFmt] ; readFileSize uses an internal format (can't set rsi)
mov rdi, [totalBytes] ; get total accumulated file size
call printFileSize ; and display as string
putchar LF

mov rdi, nRecords
call traverseList ; print the list
call freeList

.exit:
mov rdi, dir
closedir ; closrdir(dir)
putchar LF

epilogue EXIT_SUCCESS

;======================== READ-ONLY DATA SECTION ========================
section .rodata
this_dir db ".", EOL
```

```
parent_dir db "..", EOL
errFmt db "ERROR: %s is not a valid file or directory!", LF, EOL
path_sep db "/", EOL
totalFmt db "total ", EOL
usageErr db "ERROR: Did you mean to call myls?", LF, EOL

;====================== UNINITIALIZED DATA SECTION ======================
section .bss
path resb PATH_MAX

;==========================================================================
```

In fileSize.asm, if the file size is below 1K, we display it as is. The function readFileSize then performs a modulo operation in order to determine whether a floating point division is required. If the result of the modulo operation is zero, then we can simply perform an integer division.

Don't forget: for the floating point division, you must use the xmm registers as follows:

```
.nonIntegerDivide:        ; perform the floating point division
     movsd xmm0, nSize
     movsd xmm1, nDividend
     divsd xmm0, xmm1
```

See ~/Development/asm_x86_64/fileInfo/fileSize.c to help you understand how fileSize.asm works. Build the myll executable using the provided Makefile and execute myll.

```
suse-tw-z4@~/Development/asm_x86_64/directory/myll$ ./myll
total 202.1K
-rw-r--r-- 1 js users     0 Sep 16 16:20 .debug
drwxr-xr-x 8 js users  4.1K Sep 10 19:43 .git
-rw-r--r-- 1 js users    51 Sep 15 13:51 .gitignore
drwxr-xr-x 2 js users  4.1K Aug 18 15:10 .vscode
-rwxr-xr-x 1 js users 26.6K Aug 21 14:10 fileInfo*
-rw-r--r-- 1 js users  8.7K Sep 15 14:03 fileInfo.asm
-rw-r--r-- 1 js users  4.3K Aug 21 14:10 fileInfo.c
-rw-r--r-- 1 js users  8.4K Sep 16 16:20 fileInfo.obj
```

```
drwxr-xr-x 2 js users  4.1K Aug 29 15:44 files
-rw-r--r-- 1 js users  3.9K Aug 23 14:35 fileSize.asm
-rw-r--r-- 1 js users  4.2K Sep 16 16:20 fileSize.obj
-rw-r--r-- 1 js users  1.7K Aug 21 14:52 fileTime.asm
-rw-r--r-- 1 js users  3.2K Sep 16 16:20 fileTime.obj
-rw-r--r-- 1 js users  5.5K Aug 11 15:02 listTools.asm
-rw-r--r-- 1 js users  5.8K Sep 16 16:20 listTools.obj
-rwxr-xr-x 1 js users 23.9K Aug 18 06:36 lstat*
-rw-r--r-- 1 js users  2.5K Aug 17 16:53 lstat.c
-rw-r--r-- 1 js users  7.7K Sep 16 16:02 macro.inc
-rw-r--r-- 1 js users  1.9K Sep  8 16:57 Makefile
-rw-r--r-- 1 js users   707 Jul 23 15:14 maketest.sh
-rwxr-xr-x 1 js users 28.5K Sep 16 16:20 myll*
-rw-r--r-- 1 js users  4.5K Sep 16 16:20 myll.asm
-rw-r--r-- 1 js users  5.4K Sep 16 16:20 myll.obj
-rw-r--r-- 1 js users   131 Sep 15 13:52 myls.code-workspace
-rw-r--r-- 1 js users  2.2K Aug 25 12:29 quicksortStr.asm
-rw-r--r-- 1 js users  4.0K Sep 16 16:20 quicksortStr.obj
-rwxr-xr-x 1 js users 29.4K Aug  9 17:18 runLL*
-rw-r--r-- 1 js users   408 Aug 25 12:03 test.c
-rw-r--r-- 1 js users  1.4K Aug 21 17:39 test.s
-rw-r--r-- 1 js users  4.7K Jul 23 15:19 testDir.asm
lrwxrwxrwx 1 js users     4 Sep  8 16:59 theExe -> myll*
```

Activities

1. What happens if you remove the usageErr and the jump to .exit in myll.asm

2. Remove the code that prints usageErr and modify myll.asm so that it can look up file *metadata* in any arbitrary directory. Add --dir=<start_dir> command line argument to myll.asm as part of your implementation.

3. Modify readFileSize to return the number of bytes consumed by the file on disk. The value you want to convert is `stat64.st_blocks * stat64.st_blocksize`. Does this match the file size returned by \ls -lhAF?

4. Implement make install for your project. This should copy myll to /usr/local/bin.

CHAPTER 17

Reading File and Directory Information with the Help of the Linux Shell Scripting Language, BASH

In Chapter 16, we used tried and true methods for reading, characterizing, and sorting file metadata. We first open a directory and then read the files and directories inside the directory, until fileread returns NULL. This metadata extraction and decoding comprised the files fileInfo.asm, fileSize.asm, and fileTime.asm.

The processing is performed by myll.asm. We're now going to graft a new front end onto our program which will read the command line input. The new program is called myls. If we find two or more command line arguments (e.g., ./myls *.*), we'll use bash to retrieve and sort the raw information and then invoke myls to display it. We then employ the glibc function execl to execute myll. As usual, I've wrapped the invocation to execl in a couple of macros in the included file macro.inc.

The source file myls.asm is shown in Listing 17-1. Listing 17-2 shows where we added the glibc execl function to the macro.inc include file.

J. Schwartzman, *Assembly Language Reimagined*, https://doi.org/10.1007/979-8-8688-1724-3_17

Listing 17-1. myls.asm

```
;==========================================================================
; myls.asm - retrieve file metadata from useer and display as ls -lAFh
; John Schwartzman, Forte Systems, Inc.
; Fri Oct 11 05:17:25 PM EDT 2024
; linux x86_64
;
;========================== CONSTANT DEFINITIONS ==========================

%include "macro.inc"

NUM_VAR      equ     4            ; num local var main (round up to
even num)

;======================= DEFINE LOCAL VARIABLES main =====================
%define      nIndex    qword [rsp + VAR_SIZE * (NUM_VAR - 4)]    ; rsp +  0
%define      argc      qword [rsp + VAR_SIZE * (NUM_VAR - 3)]    ; rsp +  8
%define      argv0     qword [rsp + VAR_SIZE * (NUM_VAR - 2)]    ; rsp + 16
%define      nRecords  qword [rsp + VAR_SIZE * (NUM_VAR - 1)]    ; rsp + 24

;============================ CODE SECTION ===============================
section     .text
global      main
extern      fileName
extern      readFileInfo, readFileSize, printFileSize
extern      quicksortStr
extern      insertNode, traverseList, freeList
extern      listIndex
extern      totalBytes

;==========================================================================
main:
      prologue    NUM_VAR

      mov      argc, rdi                           ; argc  = rdi (1st arg
                                                     to main)
      mov      argv0, rsi                          ; argv0 = rsi (2nd arg
                                                     to main)
```

```
    cmp     argc, ONE                       ; if there is 1 arg
                                              execute myll
    jne     .continue                       ; otherwise execute myls
                                              argv0 ...

    execl   [runLLPath], [runLLArgs]        ; invoke myll
    jz      .fin                            ; jump if execl was
                                              successful

    perror [execlName]                      ; report error
    jmp     .fin                            ;     and get out

.continue:
    zero    rax
    mov     nRecords, rax                   ; nRecords = 0
    inc     rax
    mov     nIndex, rax                     ; nIndex = 1

    getcwd [path], 256                      ; get current working
                                              directory
    test   rax, rax                         ; success?
    jnz    .argvLoop                        ; jump if yes
                                            ; set path to current
                                              working directory
    perror [getcwdName]                     ; return errno
    jmp    .fin                             ; and get out

.argvLoop:                                  ; expand wildcards - do-
                                              while loop

    mov    rsi, nIndex
    mov    rax, argv0
    mov    rsi, [rax + rsi * ARG_SIZE]    ; filename - rsi =>
                                            argv[nIndex]
    lea    rdi, [fileName]
    strcpy                                ; rdi -> fileName

    mov    rcx, nRecords
    push   rcx
```

```
    call    insertFile                          ; add file metadata to list
    pop     rcx

    inc     nRecords                            ; nRecords++
    inc     nIndex                              ; nIndex++
    inc     rcx
    mov     rax, nIndex
    cmp     rax, argc                           ; nIndex == argc?
    jl      .argvLoop                           ; jump if no - END OF
                                                  .argvLoop

    mov     rdi, argc
    dec     rdi
    call    traverseList
    call    freeList

.fin:
    putchar   LF
    zero      eax
    epilogue  eax                               ; end of main

;=========================================================================
insertFile:                                     ; rcx = record number
     prologue                                   ; create new node and insert
                                                  at front of list

    lea      rsi, [fileName]                    ; get file name
    push     rcx
    call     readFileInfo                       ; read file metadata
    pop      rcx

    push     rcx
    call     insertNode                         ; create new element - rsi =>
                                                  array[rcx]

    pop      rcx
    inc      rcx
    mov      nRecords, rcx

    epilogue
```

```
;========================== READ-ONLY DATA SECTION ========================
section         .rodata
getcwdName      db          "getcwd returned", EOL
execlName       db          "execl returned", EOL
runLLPath       db          "/home/js/Development/asm_x86_64/myll/myll", EOL

;======================== UNINITIALIZED DATA SECTION ======================
section.bss
runLLArgs       db          EOL, EOL
path            resb        256

;==========================================================================
```

Listing 17-2. Excerpt from the latest macro.inc Include Module

```
%macro execl 0                                  ; execute a program
      call      execl                           ; invoke execl
      test      eax, eax                        ; execl successful (ZF = = 1)?
%endmacro

%macro execl 1
      lea       rdi, %1                         ;  path of executable
      execl
%endmacro

%macro execl 2
      lea      rdi, %1                          ; path of executable
      lea      rsi, %2                          ; command line argument
      execl
%endmacro
```

Activities

1. Reorganize myls.asm so that it doesn't invoke myll, but performs all of the necessary activities itself.
2. Write the macro instructions that would allow execl to take additional run time arguments. Demonstrate that it works.

3. What is a *varadic* instruction?

4. Copy myls and myll to /usr/local/bin so that they will always be accessible from the CLI. Don't forget to change the `runLLPath` variable in myls.asm. Add a make install target to Makefile to make the release version of myls.

5. What is the meaning of the Linux shell command `which myls`?

6. What is the meaning of the Linux shell command `which myll`?

7. What is the meaning of the Linux shell command `which ./myls`?

8. Modify myls.asm so that it chooses a different execution path if the myls main function only wants to find the file metadata in a specific directory. Use $ `myls -dir=<start_dir>`.

Afterword

This book is based on first principles. You have learned what the CPU can do and what it can't, and how it accomplishes what it can do. You have learned about the logic gates inside the CPU and how they're used to change the order of execution of a program.

Assembly language is closely tied to the C programming language. Much of what we accomplished was by calling various methods of the C runtime library. We used C programs to call assembly language modules, and we used assembly language programs that had main subroutines inside them. These modules did some work in assembly language, but more often than not, they called C methods and functions to do the actual work.

We saw how the operating system uses the C Calling Convention to pass arguments to assembly language programs and to C Programs. We saw which registers were used to pass these arguments. We also saw how C and assembly languages returned control to the operating system automatically, by exiting the main method. We saw that the main methods returned status information too. We saw how the stack and the heap memory allocations are used. We saw how metadata is found and stored and how this metadata is sorted and searched.

Above all, we saw that the C library consists of statements, structures, initializations, and tests that are written in assembly language. Every kind of programming language ultimately runs assembly language on the CPU.

What's next? Your next goal is to find out about where and how assembly language is used. We usually dig out assembly language when we're faced with a problem that needs assembly language: when we don't have enough memory, or we have enough memory, but we need more speed. Programs that handle visual effects in medical imagery are often good targets for assembly language. Finding out what malware is doing often requires disassembly of embedded code using a debugger. We're told that the radar target acquisition subsystem of a modern fighter aircraft can have programs with upward of two billion lines of real-time code. Some of that code is a good target for assembly language. Many of these kinds of problems can be modeled and solved by linear algebra. Implementing the solving of these systems of equations is a job that can by well suited to assembly language.

J. Schwartzman, *Assembly Language Reimagined*, https://doi.org/10.1007/979-8-8688-1724-3

The x64 CPU has the AVX, AVX2, and AVX-512 subsystems that are well suited to the rapid solution of these types of problems. Daniel Kusswurm covers these subsystems in depth in *Modern X86 Assembly Language Programming,* Third Edition (Apress, 2023).

If you're interested in programming for Microsoft Windows, check out *The Art of 64-Bit Assembly,* by Randall Hyde (No Starch Press, 2022).

You might consider learning the RUST programming language. RUST has safer memory allocations than does C, and RUST is now included in the Linux kernel.

Please keep experimenting with assembly language. Try things. Change things. Good luck and have fun!

APPENDIX A

Installing the Software

We're going to install gcc, gdb, make, git, and valgrind. On my openSUSE distro, I issued the command

```
$ sudo zypper install gcc gdb make git valgrind
```

On Ubuntu or similar distros you can issue the command

```
$ sudo apt install gcc gdb make git valgrind
```

I like the convenience of Microsoft Visual Studio Code's integration with git, but you can use any simple text editor that you like. Word processing editors like Microsoft Word or Libre Office Writer are not appropriate for writing source code. Simple text editors or programming editors are the tools that you'll need.

To install Visual Studio Code

Point your browser to `https://code.visualstudio.com/docs/?dv=linux64_rpm` and see if your distro offers to install it for you. If it does, you're finished, otherwise try the next step.

In your Downloads directory, issue the command

```
$ sudo rpm -ivh code-1.86.1-1707298208.el8.x86_64.rpm
```

To install DDD

1. Download the tarball located at `http://ftp.gnu.org/gnu/ddd/`
2. In your Downloads directory, issue the following command to extract the files and directories from the tarball.

   ```
   $ tar xfz ddd-<version>.tar.gz
   ```

   It may be necessary to download and install some additional packages before you can build DDD. I needed to install motif-devel, libXt-devel, libXaw-devel, and libXm-devel using my distro's package manager.

J. Schwartzman, *Assembly Language Reimagined*, https://doi.org/10.1007/979-8-8688-1724-3

3. Executing configure will tell you what else is necessary to build DDD from source.

4. Issue the following commands in the Downloads directory.

`$ tar xfz ddd-<version>.tar.gz`	This will extract the tarball.
`$ mkdir build`	This will create a build directory.
`$ cd build`	This will set ~/Downloads/build as the PWD.

5. Configure DDD

   The following command will prepare the DDD project for building the ddd executable in the /usr/local directory.

   ```
   $ ../ddd-<version>/configure
   ```

   This may issue warnings about missing libraries or support programs.

   Install any missing programs using your distro's package manager, and then rerun configure until it issues the following:

   ```
   "configuration is done.  Type `make` to compile DDD."
   ```

6. Build DDD

   At the command prompt, enter

   ```
   js@suse-tumbleweed-z4:~/Downloads/build$ sudo make install
   ```

   You should now be finished. If make doesn't report any errors then type "ddd" to see if the DDD debugger executes. If you're using more than one monitor, make sure that your additional monitor is turned on since DDD will normally write to the secondary monitor.

   ```
   $ ddd
   ```

7. With DDD running, select Edit ➤ Preferences ➤ Source and press "Display Source Line Numbers".
8. Set tab width to 4.
9. With DDD running, Select Edit ➤ Preferences ➤ Startup and press Keyboard Focus to "Click To Type".
10. These preferences will be saved by DDD in its configuration file.

Download the source code for this textbook:

```
$ git clone x64srcRepository into ~/Development
```

Glossary

ABI ABI stands for Application Binary Interface. It is a set of hardware-specific rules that allow different pieces of software to communicate with one another.

abstraction Abstraction refers to the hiding of detail. High-level languages hide the details of the computer hardware from the programmer. Assembly language throws the details right back in your face.

algorithm An algorithm is a technique or recipe for solving a problem. Algorithms are translated into programming languages.

alias An alias is an abbreviation for a Linux command. It can also include command line options, and it is used in the command line interface (CLI). The statement \command will execute the unaliased version of command.

API API stands for Application Programming Interface. It is a set of defined rules that enable different pieces of application software to communicate with each other.

argument An argument is a value that the caller of a method or function passes to the method or function. Subroutines can take many arguments.

artifact An artifact is something that is made. An output file produced by make is an artifact.

ASCII ASCII is a collection of characters in the American Standard Code for Information Interchange.

ASCIIZ ASCIIZ is a NULL (Zero) terminated ASCII string.

big-endian Processors that use big-endian format place the most significant byte in the higher address and the least significant byte in the lower address. (See little-endian.)

J. Schwartzman, *Assembly Language Reimagined*, https://doi.org/10.1007/979-8-8688-1724-3

BIOS BIOS stands for Basic Input Output Services. It is an interface provided by the operating system that allows programs to access peripheral devices. The BIOS performs the Power On Self Test (POST) and loads the operating system.

bit A bit is a single binary digit. It can have the value zero or one.

Boolean A branch of algebra dealing with logical operations (AND, OR, NOT, etc.). There are two possible states for a Boolean operation. These states are known as FALSE or TRUE, commonly known as 0 or 1. Boolean algebra is named after George Boole, who first defined it in the mid nineteenth century.

byte A byte is 8-bits of memory.

cache A cache is computer memory with very short access time used for storage of frequently or recently used instructions or data. Cache is built into the CPU. Accessing the cache is faster than RAM, so more cache can greatly improve CPU performance.

character A character is a letter or number represented in ASCII.

CISC CISC stands for Complex Instruction Set Computer. A CISC implements complex instructions as opcodes rather than relying on software. See RISC.

CLI CLI stands for the Command Line Interface. It is a tool for interfacing with a program that uses text commands. When we type make, we type it at the CLI.

computer A computer consists of one or more CPUs, RAM and ROM memory, address and data busses, and peripherals.

CPU The CPU is the Central Processing Unit of a computer. It is the arithmetic and logic portion of a computer. It contains many special-purpose and general-purpose registers.

CWD The CWD is the Current Working Directory, which is also known as the Present Working Directory, PWD.

DDD DDD is the Data Display Debugger program. It is a GUI front-end to GDB (the gnu debugger).

dqueue A dqueue (pronounced deck) is a double-ended queue data structure.

de rigueur De rigueur means a strict requirement or a convention to be observed.

distro Distro stands for a Linux distribution like Ubuntu, SUSE, Fedora, etc.

doubleword A doubleword is 4-bytes or 32-bits of memory.

double quadword A double quadword is 16-bytes or 128-bits of memory.

function A function is a subroutine that returns a value. All glibc subroutines return a value and are therefore functions.

gdb gdb is the gnu debugger. It is a tool that lets you single-step through a program, examine registers, variables, data, etc. gdb has a CLI. DDD is a GUI front-end for gdb.

glibc glibc is the GNU C run-time Library. Assembly language programs make extensive use of glibc. You should use glibc to access BIOS methods.

GNU's Not UNIX GNU is a Unix-like operating system. That means it is a collection of many programs: applications, libraries and developer tools. The development of GNU, started in January 1984, is known as the GNU Project. Many of the programs in GNU are released under the auspices of the GNU Project; those we call GNU packages.

GPU A GPU is a Graphics Processing Unit. It is a special-purpose CPU for graphical operations.

GUI GUI stands for Graphical User Interface. It is an image-based interface to a computer program.

heap A heap is a dynamically resizable region of memory used for memory allocations by your program. In an object-oriented programming language, the heap is where instances of user-defined objects (classes) are stored.

IO IO stands for input/output. It is the process of writing a value to a peripheral device by the CPU, or reading a value from a peripheral device by the CPU.

label A label is the target of a conditional or unconditional jump in assembly language. It represents a memory address.

Linux Linux is an open source, UNIX-like multi-user operating system.

little-endian The format that Intel uses for adding bytes to memory or registers is called little-endian. In little-endian processors, the least significant byte goes into the lower address and the most significant byte goes into the higher address.

macro A macro is a recipe for invoking assembly language instructions. Macros can be overloaded based on the number of arguments they take.

marshal To marshal is to organize and make ready for action. When calling a subroutine, any arguments to the subroutine are marshaled in registers or on the stack.

metadata Metadata is information about data. The Linux bash shell catalogs and sorts information about file and directory ownership, permissions, size, and time. This is metadata from the files found in a directory on a drive.

method A method is the code at a location designated by a label. The method is accessed by the CALL label instruction. The method ends with the RET instruction, which causes the instruction pointer register (rip) to be set with the return address which was placed on the stack by the call instruction. A method is a subroutine that does not return a value, as opposed to a function, which does return a value.

Mnemonic A mnemonic is simple name or abbreviation given to numeric machine language instructions. It is a memory aid.

nibble A nibble is 4-bits of memory (half a byte).

non-volatile Non-volatile means it does not change easily. Memory like ROM holds its value even when the computer is powered off. (See volatile.)

op code An op code is a basic machine language instruction of a CPU.

order The order of an algorithm shows its comparative speed. Order progresses from constant time to n (where n is the number of elements to process), to n log n, to n^2, ….

OS An OS (operating system) is the software that controls a computer. It performs memory allocation and deallocation. It loads, starts, unloads, and ends programs. It performs input and output to computer hardware peripherals. Linux, Apple OS X, and Microsoft Windows 11 are three common operating systems used on personal computers.

OS X A closed source operating system (OS) used to execute multiuser programs on an Apple computer.

parameter Inside a called method or function, we refer to the arguments to the method or function as parameters.

POSIX POSIX stands for Portable Operating System Interface function. Glibc establishes a set of POSIX functions that provide low-level access to system resources.

program A program consists of hundreds, thousands, millions, or billions of machine language instructions organized to perform specified tasks.

prompt A prompt is some text that tells the user that a command line interface (*CLI*) is ready for input. The CLI usually presents a $ symbol followed by a blinking cursor as a prompt.

PWD The Present Working Directory is also known as the Current Working Directory, CWD. When you type \ls with no arguments, you see the contents of the PWD.

qbyte A qbyte or quad-byte is 8-bytes or 64-bits of memory. It can represent a numeric value or a memory address.

queue A queue is a FIFO data structure used to hold data for a computer program.

RAM RAM stands for Random Access Memory, which is memory that is both readable and writable.

recursion Recursion is when a function calls itself.

register A register is a small, fast, named memory location inside the CPU of a computer. Registers may be general purpose (rax, rbx, rsi, rdi, etc.) or specific to a certain function (rip, rsp, rflags, etc.). Registers in the x86_64 are 64-bits in length, but there are also addressable 32-bit, 16-bit, and 8-bit registers.

RISC RISC stands for Reduced Instruction Set Computer. A RISC will rely on software for the implementation of complex instructions. RISC will only implement instructions in hardware that can run in a limited number of clock cycles. See CISC.

ROM ROM stands for read-only memory, which is memory that can be read but not written.

shared library A shared library is a program that can be loaded into memory and accessed by many other programs. Glibc (libc.so.6) is an example of a shared library. Shared libraries are a common way to distribute software.

stack A stack is an area of memory that is accessed by the rsp register. It is a LIFO data structure. Every running program is given its own stack by Linux.

string A string is an ordered collection of ASCII characters. A C string must be terminated with a zero byte (ASCIIZ).

structured program statements High-level languages supply easy-to-use structures. They include statements like if, else if, else, for, do-while, while-do, and switch-case. Assembly language lacks these structures and we must work hard to translate structures into assembly language. An in-depth knowledge of structure statements, conditions, and tests is necessary for all programmers.

subroutine Both methods and functions are subroutines. When the CPU's instruction pointer (rip) encounters a ret statement in the subroutine code, the return address is popped from the stack and the CPU executes the code following the call statement. The CPU pushes the return address onto the stack when the CPU's instruction pointer encounters a call instruction.

UEFI UEFI stands for Unified Extensible Firmware Interface. It is an open source replacement for the *BIOS*. The BIOS or the *UEFI* are available as soon as the computer is powered on. They provide access to the hardware peripherals, perform the Power On Self Test (POST), and load the operating system.

varadic A varadic function or method has a variable number of arguments. The function will determine the exact number of arguments at runtime.

volatile Volatile means readily changeable. RAM is volatile and ROM is non-volatile. That is, ROM retains its value even after the computer is turned off, while RAM powers on to an unknown state.

Windows A closed source operating system (OS) used to execute multiuser programs on a Microsoft-based computer or on a Microsoft clone computer.

word A word represents 2 bytes or 16-bits of memory. Sometimes word size is used to specify an amount of memory that is processor dependent. For example, in the original Intel 8086 microprocessor, the word size was stated to be 16-bits. In the Intel 80386 microprocessor, the word size was stated to be 32-bits.

OP CODES

malloc instruction (allocate memory in the heap)	89
free instruction (release memory allocation from the heap)	95
lea instruction (load effective address)	10
mov instruction (move)	10, 45
cmovz instruction - conditional-move-if-zero (move if ZF = 1)	55, 58
call instruction	23, 38
ret instruction1	5, 35

Endnotes

[1] Brian W. Kernighan and Dennis M. Ritchie famously introduced the C language in their 1978 book *The C Programming Language*, with a program that printed "Hello, world".

Kernighan, B.W., and Ritchie, D.M. *The C Programming Language*, first edition (Englewood Cliffs, New Jersey: Prentice Hall, 1978).

Kernighan, B.W., and Ritchie, D.M. *The C Programming Language*, second edition (Englewood Cliffs, New Jersey: Prentice Hall, 1988).

[2] Analog (analogue) computers are a useful engineering tool for modeling circuit behavior in the laboratory. For practical purposes, we use digital computers to find answers to problems.

[3] An application binary interface (ABI) is a set of rules specifying how a binary executable should exchange information with some service (e.g., the kernel or a library) at runtime. Among other things, an ABI specifies which registers and stack locations are used to exchange this information, and what meaning is attached to the exchanged values. Once compiled for a particular ABI, a binary executable should be able to run on any system presenting the same ABI.

Kerrisk, M., *The Linux Programming Interface* (San Francisco, California: No Starch Press, 2010).

J. Schwartzman, *Assembly Language Reimagined*, https://doi.org/10.1007/979-8-8688-1724-3

[4] An application programming interface (API) is a set of defined rules that enable different applications to communicate with each other. It acts as an intermediary layer that processes data transfers between systems.

An API guarantees portability only for applications compiled from source code.

`https://www.ibm.com/topics/api`.

[5] University of Oxford, Department of Computer Science.

Index

A

Alias, 41, 183

B

Boolean logic gates, 20–21, 23

C, D, E

Conditional build, 67–75
Conditional compilation, 67–75, 84
Creating and sorting a linked list, 165–182

F, G

File and directory operations, 51, 157–164, 183–213, 215–220
Floating point registers, 87–93
Footnotes

H, I, J, K, L

Heap, 9, 221

M, N

Makefile, 1, 3, 5–10, 15, 19, 33, 36, 37, 41, 64, 65, 67, 71, 83, 84, 103, 110, 112, 113, 118, 120, 121, 128, 135, 152, 163, 164, 166, 179, 181, 211, 220
Mnemonics, 129

O

Order (Big O notation), 123

P, Q

Programs
  bsortInt.c, 124
  bubblesortInt.asm, 126, 128, 129, 135, 178
  bubblesortStr.asm, 142, 152, 178, 185
  cmdline.asm, 30, 43, 44, 50, 52, 92
  cmdline.c, 43, 47, 50
  commaSeparate.asm, 96, 102, 113
  dir.asm, 159, 163, 164, 166, 178, 179
  dir.c, 157
  environment.asm, 55, 56, 61, 64
  environment.c, 55, 60
  factorial.asm, 77, 79
  factorial.c, 77, 113, 116, 118, 119
  hello.asm, 1, 2, 6, 7, 13, 40
  hello.c, 1, 2, 5–7, 40
  hhmmss.asm, 106, 112, 113
  hhmmss.cpp, 117, 118, 120
  listTools.asm, 165, 166, 171, 178, 179
  llDir.asm, 166, 178, 179
  minmax.asm, 67, 69, 73
  minmax.c, 67, 75
  qsortInt.asm
  qsortInt.c, 129, 130, 135
  qsortStr.c, 145
  quicksortInt.asm, 129, 130, 178, 179
  quicksortStr.asm, 140, 152, 178, 179, 185

J. Schwartzman, *Assembly Language Reimagined*, https://doi.org/10.1007/979-8-8688-1724-3

R

Recursion, 77–85
Recursive programming
  factorial, 77, 83–85, 95, 102, 103, 120
  Fibonacci Series, 120
  quicksort, 129, 130, 132, 135, 145, 147, 150

S

Shared libraries, 113–121
Shell scripts, 1, 6, 9, 35, 38–40, 135, 151, 215–220
Sorting an array of integers, 123–137
Sorting an array of strings, 139–156
Stack, 9, 29–31, 37, 48, 55–65, 74, 84, 85, 166, 182, 221

T

The C Calling Convention, 29, 31–32, 221
The Linker (gcc), 6, 32–37, 40, 48, 67, 113
The loader (ld), 6, 37

U, V, W, X, Y, Z

Using glibc instead of using the BIOS directly, 29–41
Using macros to extend assembly language, 62
Using the BIOS for I/O, 1–13

GPSR Compliance
The European Union's (EU) General Product Safety Regulation (GPSR) is a set of rules that requires consumer products to be safe and our obligations to ensure this.

If you have any concerns about our products, you can contact us on

ProductSafety@springernature.com

In case Publisher is established outside the EU, the EU authorized representative is:

Springer Nature Customer Service Center GmbH
Europaplatz 3
69115 Heidelberg, Germany

www.ingramcontent.com/pod-product-compliance
Lightning Source LLC
LaVergne TN
LVHW081449060526
838201LV00050BA/1747
* 9 7 9 8 8 6 8 8 1 7 2 3 6 *